Beyond Words

An introduction, guide and resource
for a contemplative way of prayer

PATRICK WOODHOUSE

First published in 2001 by
KEVIN MAYHEW LTD
Buxhall
Stowmarket
Suffolk IP14 3BW

© 2001 Patrick Woodhouse

0 1 2 3 4 5 6 7 8 9

ISBN 1 84003 691 5
Catalogue No 1500409

Cover design by Jonathan Stroulger
Edited and typeset by Margaret Lambeth

CONTENTS

About the author

Patrick Woodhouse is the Canon Precentor of Wells Cathedral. Prior to moving to Wells, he was the Vicar of St Andrew's, Chippenham, in Wiltshire, and before that he worked in the Church of England's ministry of Social Responsibility as Adviser in the Dioceses of Winchester and Carlisle. He is author of *In Search of the Kingdom* (Marshall-Pickering, 1989). He is married to Sam, a teacher who works in the field of world development education, and they have two grown-up daughters.

Acknowledgements

Most of this book was written amidst the demands and activities of a busy Church of England parish, and in the last year of my time as parish priest of St Andrew's, Chippenham. I would like to express my thanks to many friends and colleagues in the St Andrew's community for their support. Special thanks are due to two people who commented in detail on a draft of the manuscript, and for whose friendship and creative interest I am particularly grateful: Michael Sammes, a member of St Andrew's; and Brother Bernard of the Society of Saint Francis.

As this book has taken shape, I have drawn on the long tradition of contemplative spirituality and I am indebted to the writings of many that have travelled far further than I have on this road. I would particularly like to mention Olivier Clément's *The Roots of Christian Mysticism* which became for me a constant companion as, drawing on the roots of tradition, I tried to map out in quite practical and experiential terms something of what it means to explore prayer in a more contemplative way. I commend it to the reader.

Finally, my greatest debt of thanks is to my wife Sam, whose clarity of perception and warmth of encouragement has, as always, been a constant inspiration. This book is dedicated to her with much love and gratitude.

PREFACE

This introduction and guide to the practice of contemplative prayer is written in the hope that it will encourage and help all who, like me, find the challenge of praying in the modern world difficult.

If we believe in God, then to pray must be the most important challenge we face. Yet it *is* somehow hugely difficult – at least I have found it so. I guess that large numbers of people must also feel that, and like me will have made intermittent stabs at it and then, lacking the right kind of encouragement and help, have perhaps given up.

As a young student at University I was drawn into the search for a faith that would make sense, and ever since I have floundered around with this business of trying to pray. It has always seemed to me to be the key question – more to do with the fascinating *how* of belief rather than the more ponderous *what*.

After going down various blind alleys, and for long periods of time more or less leaving it behind altogether, a clearer idea began to emerge as to what might be needed and a deeper sense as to just what prayer both is and is not.

I can trace four key influences that have helped shape these emerging understandings:

Firstly, involvement in the early 1970s with Dr Frank Lake and the work of the Clinical Theology Association and subsequent experience in various kinds of psychotherapy. This took me below the surface and helped me to begin to understand something of the crucial links between belief and the more hidden workings of the mind.

Then I owe a huge debt to the Anglican Franciscan community where, twenty-five years ago, I first met a community of people who really took prayer seriously.

And then, in 1981, I bought a book about an American monk called Thomas Merton of whom I knew nothing at all. It began a very significant relationship with someone whose writings have opened up the tradition of contemplative prayer – both Christian and that of other faiths – making that tradition accessible. I felt especially close to him in

1997 when on a period of study leave; I was fortunate to be able to visit the Indian subcontinent and go to Pollonaruwa in Sri Lanka and sit before the huge and beautiful statues of the Buddha that Merton wrote about so movingly and graphically in his *Asian Journal*. This was just a few days before he died.

Finally, in recent years I have been grateful for the systematic teaching of a method of meditation given through the International Community of Christian Meditation founded by Fr John Main.

Slowly these influences, and the rich tradition of contemplative prayer that they point to, have given some shape and direction to my own efforts at praying. However, the more this tradition has helped me, the more I have become aware that it still remains obscure, hidden, and still somehow inaccessible for most church people, just at the time when, in the Anglican Church at least, it is so very badly needed.

It is for this reason that I have written this introduction and guide to a contemplative way of praying. I hope that it will help others to gain access to a tradition and a way of prayer that I have personally found hugely valuable. I believe the present-day Church is most profoundly in need of this tradition.

We are meant to pray. To the extent that a person stops praying, something at the heart of human identity is dying in that individual.

Jim Forest [1]

INTRODUCTION

Beyond Words is in three parts:

Chapter 1 – The Challenge of Praying

The opening chapter begins to explore what is meant by contemplative prayer, and why it matters so much. It touches on some of the difficulties of praying in this way in the secular culture of the modern world.

Chapters 2 and 3 – What do I need? *and* What do I do?

These two chapters offer a practical guide to actually starting to pray. Chapter 2 explores four essentials without which no life of prayer can grow. Chapter 3 suggests that the time given to prayer needs to be focused in three ways –

- time for becoming still
- time for the offering of life
- time for reflection

These chapters look in detail at each of these ways of using time. This part of the book ends with some practical points before embarking on the weekly guide.

The weekly guide

A guide and programme to help the reader enter into a contemplative approach to prayer week by week throughout the Church's year using the Gospel readings for Year C of the Common Worship Lectionary, the Year of Luke.

A contemplative approach

Throughout the guide, the hope is to foster a way of contemplation. To contemplate should not be thought of as some kind of strange esoteric practice; it simply means to see – to see what really is, and to wonder:

'Cleansing the doors of perception,' said William Blake, 'reveals everything as it truly is – infinite.'[2]

'Come and see' is the repeated invitation of the Gospel of John.

St Augustine reminds us that the whole purpose of this life is to restore to health the eye of the heart whereby God may be seen.[3]

In producing this guide, the hope is that however the reader understands prayer they will at least begin, or begin again, using this guide for what it is – a rough guide only. There is no intention to impose a fixed pattern; prayer can never be like that. Each of us, led by the Spirit, must discover for ourselves our own unique pattern that will be shaped by our very particular histories and circumstances and personalities.

But the important thing is to BEGIN! – or to realise that we will always be beginning again. 'Our ascent is unending' said Gregory of Nyssa, one of the great Fathers of the Church. 'We go from beginning to beginning by way of beginnings without end.'[4]

> Not everything has a name. Some things lead us into the realm beyond words . . . It is like that small mirror in the fairy-tales . . . You glance in it and what you see is not yourself; for an instant you glimpse the Inaccessible, where no horse or magic carpet can take you. And the soul cries out for it.
>
> Alexander Solzhenitsyn [5]

CHAPTER 1 THE CHALLENGE OF PRAYING

Beyond Words sets out to provide an introduction and guide to help with the most important challenge of life, namely, how to set about the task of praying on a regular basis.

Learning how to pray cannot be an optional extra for anyone who believes in the possibility of God because to pray is to seek to enter into the very presence of God. And for the person who has begun to believe, or who continues to hold to belief, nothing in life can be more important than that. Nothing can make more of a difference to how life is lived.

But it is not easy because we live in a very secular society where God is largely forgotten; not easy because our lives are so distracted.

The power of secularism

For large numbers of people outside the churches, and also within them, God is increasingly remote, less and less a part of everyday experience, in the way that he once was. This is because of the growth of secularism, the modern creed that says that human beings can get on very well in the world without any need to resort to belief in God.

Though the seeds of present-day secularism were sown way back in the eighteenth century in the period of European thought known as the 'Enlightenment', it has taken a very long time to filter through into the common mind and common assumptions of our time.

All the way through the nineteenth century and right through the first half of the twentieth century, the symbols and rituals of the Christian faith still provided society with an overarching story and set of meanings. Its feasts and seasons, prayers and teachings were, by and large, widely acknowledged, valued, and entered into. They spilt over into the language and fabric of our culture, illuminating everyday life with a sense of the reality of faith.

Until well into the second half of the twentieth century it was still possible to gain a sense of God and the meanings of faith even if you didn't go to church. In the education of children, the celebration of national rituals, the keeping of Sunday as a day of rest, the life of national institutions, and in many other ways, life was still punctuated with explicit religious references. These reminded people, even subconsciously, of the meaning to life given through the Christian story.

This is now very largely gone and church members cannot be isolated from the prevailing spirit of the times any more than anyone else. None of us lives or thinks alone. We are all part of the world around us, and are deeply and subconsciously influenced by the trends of thought which come at us through the media, and through the habits, customs, and behaviour of our fellow citizens. Our western consumerist world largely assumes that God is, if not dead, then a rather quaint irrelevance – useful for the heritage industry in terms of keeping up Cathedrals and ancient churches – but as a working hypothesis for living in the world, largely finished.

The increasingly prevalent assumption of our times is that the sciences, both natural (biology, physics, chemistry, and now genetics) and behavioural (psychiatry and psychoanalysis), have made God redundant. Many would now assume he belongs to an essentially medieval world view, from whose superstitions and beliefs science has steadily set us free. They would say that the era of religion, as traditionally understood, is now essentially past – at least in the western world. It simply no longer fits the scientific understanding of the world that now holds sway.

So, in the public mind of our society, the tide of faith has steadily ebbed, particularly over the last fifty years, until it has now almost entirely gone from sight. And as it has ebbed, the regular practice of a living faith has become increasingly difficult, even for those who still regularly set out to worship. While God may still be an idea loyally held to in the mind, in terms of experience he will become more and more marginal unless strong commitments are entered into that counter this all-pervasive mood of secular scepticism.

In short, there is a need to find ways and practices that will nourish the forgotten potential of faith, and will lead not to mere sentimental and superficial piety but to what faith has always pointed to – the beautifying of all human life, energising and transforming it into something graceful, glorious and full of promise.

This guide attempts to explore what such ways and practices might mean, and what disciplines might be needed to sustain them amidst the very practical demands of modern life. It is about trying to rediscover a discipline of praying, so that rather than it being a barren and increasingly neglected obligation, as I fear is the case in the lives of many, it becomes a fruitful and potentially life-transforming challenge.

The waning of prayer

I suspect that in the minds of many church people, particularly those who don't belong to a simple evangelical persuasion, 'prayer' is a word that increasingly makes us feel uncomfortable. As loyal church members, we know we are *supposed* to pray; it should be at the heart of the life of Christian people. But in truth it is probably not being done very much, and we may well feel that we are no longer at all sure how to. Perhaps at the beginning of Lent or at the Easter season, or after an inspiring sermon, new efforts are made. However, because it is still largely assumed that prayer requires many words, the likelihood is that efforts will tail off again as the words used somehow prove insufficient to express inarticulate longings and needs that are more deeply within us.

People have difficulties with prayer for many reasons. These may spring from fundamental doubts about the whole meaning of faith, and whether God is not indeed an outdated illusion. Powerful voices constantly insist that this is now so, and label the whole idea of religious faith in the modern era as simply ridiculous. It is hard to remain unaffected by such assertively secular attitudes. Or they may be to do with the lifestyles of those around us. Sunday morning may be a time for many things – reading the Sunday papers, taking the kids to football, having a round of golf, or just having a long lie in and then sauntering down to the pub . . . but going to church?! In the face of this kind of indifference keeping a commitment to worship is difficult. It takes an enduring determination to go on attending church and trying to make sense of belief when the world around has so clearly given up on it.

However, I suspect that our difficulties with praying are not so much intellectual, nor even to do with going against the grain of prevailing social attitudes. The nub of the matter is, I believe, to do with praying itself: how we still try to do it, how it is still largely understood.

We probably still think of it as something akin to an extended conversation between us as subject and God as object, in which a large number of words of adoration, of confession, of thanksgiving, of supplication, seem to have to come from our side. That is how we have been taught, after all. Though we are reminded occasionally that our prayer needs to include an element of 'listening', the general assumption seems to be that prayer is, by and large, us bringing our needs, worries, thanks and hopes to the God whom we hope is somehow listening to us. And so we say our prayers, as sincerely as we can – sometimes using books of prayers, sometimes making up our own – and then we go on our way hoping that the words uttered have somehow been sufficient.

However, we may well have the sense that the words spoken have somehow remained just that – mere words spoken. No doubt we mean what we say, but in the ways of prayer that we have been taught, it is difficult to escape the feeling that the words uttered are simply emerging from an anxious surface of the mind. We do not go away either nourished or restored in spirit as we long to be. We find that our prayer is not connecting with deeper needs within us – needs that we may be only dimly aware of, but which go on being unmet and untouched, despite our prayers.

This lack of sufficient 'connectedness', means that our practice of praying can easily wither to a tired routine or an occasional special plea at a time of crisis, but little else. All too easily it degenerates into little more than dutiful obligation which becomes increasingly difficult to sustain. This, I suspect, is where many loyal church people find themselves.

However the picture is not always as bleak as this.

Moments of transcendence

Despite the power of secularism, powerful evidence for a 'spiritual dimension' to life persists, and from time to time erupts in people's experience in the most ordinary circumstances, often to their surprise and sometimes in quite overwhelming ways. It is as though, in the midst of ordinary life, glimpses are given into another world. Although what is seen is still intensely *this* world, for a fleeting moment everything is seen differently. The writer Paul Eluard wrote, 'There is another world, but it is in this one'.[6]

Sometimes, in what might be called moments of transcendence, we glimpse something of what those words mean. It is to do with our capacity to *see*. Such moments of transcendence can be very powerful, pulling people back onto the path of a spiritual search, when they feel they have all but abandoned it. Or such moments simply live on in the memory, sustaining faith when so much in the world around seems to undermine it.

Research by the Religious Experience Research Unit in Oxford has shown that such 'moments' occur to people irrespective of whether they regularly practise a religion or not; and although they may occur only perhaps once in a lifetime, such experiences are not uncommon in the population as a whole. Set up by the Professor of Zoology, Sir Alister Hardy, in 1969, this Research Unit has carried out extensive surveys of the experiences of ordinary members of the public. It has invited 'all who have been conscious of, and perhaps influenced by, some power, whether they call it the power of God or not, to write a simple but brief account of these feelings and their effects'. Thousands have responded to this invitation, and their replies show that many people do indeed have moments that might loosely be called 'mystical'. They are moments of 'seeing'.

While the accounts vary hugely, these experiences seem to have certain features in common. Firstly, the experience is usually accompanied by a profound sense of wonder and awe; then people tell of a sense of somehow being at one with the world around them, with barriers of difference between them and what is not them dissolving. A source of profound goodness and well-being seems to underlie everything, and through it all there is a deep affirmation of personal identity and worth.

This account of a childhood experience, of a young girl walking over the moors at Pangbourne as the sun set and a mist formed, demonstates these feelings:

> *Here and there just the tallest harebells appeared above the mist. I had a great love of these exquisitely formed flowers, and stood lost in wonder at the sight. Suddenly I seemed to see the mist as a shimmering gossamer tissue and the harebells, appearing here and there, seemed to shine with a brilliant fire. Somehow I understood that this was the living tissue of life itself, in which that which we call consciousness was embedded, appearing here and there as a shining focus of energy in the more*

diffused whole. In that moment I knew that I had my own special place, as had all other things, animate and so-called inanimate, and that we were all part of this universal tissue which was both fragile yet immensely strong, and utterly good and beneficent. The vision has never left me. It is as clear today as fifty years ago, and with it the same intense feeling of love of the world and the certainty of ultimate good. It gave me a strong, clear sense of identity, which has withstood many vicissitudes, and an affinity with plants, birds, animals, even insects, and people too, which has often been commented upon. Moreover, the whole of this experience has ever since formed a kind of reservoir of strength fed from an unseen source, from which quite suddenly in the midst of the very darkest times a bubble of pure joy rises through it all, and I know that whatever the anguish there is some deep centre in my life which cannot be touched by it.[7]

In his book *This Sunrise of Wonder*, in the chapter 'The Transfigured Commonplace', Michael Mayne quotes a similar experience taken from the journal of an elderly man:

One morning when I was well over sixty, I was in a wood and something happened which was nothing less than a transformation of myself and the world. All my life I had been a lover of the country, and I had believed that the same thought, spirit, life, God which was in everything I beheld, was also in me. But my creed had been taken from books . . . I was looking at a great, spreading, bursting, oak. The first tinge from the greenish-yellow buds was just visible. It seemed to be no longer a tree apart from me. The enclosing barriers of consciousness were removed, and the text came to my mind, 'Thou in me and I in thee'. . . the distinction between the self and not-self was an illusion . . . I do not argue, I cannot explain. It will be easy to prove me absurd, but nothing can shake me.[8]

In his lectures 'Re-enchanting the bourgeois mind' given in June 1998 in Wells Cathedral, Melvyn Matthews quotes a similar experience of 'at-one-ment' recorded in the diary of Admiral Byrd who manned an Antarctic weather station in 1934:

Took my daily walk at 4 pm today in 89 degrees of frost . . . I paused to listen to the silence . . . the day was dying, the night was being born, but with great peace. Here were imponderable processes and forces of the cosmos . . . harmonious and soundless. Harmony, that was it! That was what came out of the silence – a gentle rhythm, the strain of a perfect chord, the music of the spheres perhaps. It was enough to catch that rhythm, momentarily to be myself part of it. In that instant I could feel no doubt of man's oneness with the universe.[9]

A similar kind of experience happened to the monk Thomas Merton while standing in a shopping precinct in Louisville, Kentucky. It is recorded in his book *Conjectures of a Guilty Bystander* and was clearly a turning point in his life. He had fled to the Cistercian monastery of our Lady of Gethsemane in Kentucky in the winter of 1941 to seek God in the rigorous austerity of the monastic life. Nearly two decades later, in a moment of enlightenment, he realises how deeply mistaken he has been in hanging on to the world-despising attitudes that were part and parcel of monastic life at that time. He writes how one day:

In Louisville, at the corner of Fourth and Walnut, in the center of the shopping district, I was suddenly overwhelmed with the realisation that I loved all those people, that they were mine and I theirs, that we could not be alien to one another even though we were total strangers. It was like waking from a dream of separateness, of spurious self-isolation in a special world, the world of renunciation and supposed holiness. The whole illusion of a separate holy existence is a dream. Not that I question the reality of my vocation, or of my monastic life: but the conception of 'separation from the world' that we have in the monastery too easily presents itself as a complete illusion . . . we are in the same world as everybody else, the world of the bomb, the world of race hatred, the world of technology, the world of mass media, big business, revolution, and all the rest. We take a different attitude to all these things, for we belong to God. Yet so does everybody else belong to God . . . This sense of liberation from an illusory difference was such a relief and such a joy to me that I almost laughed out loud. And I suppose my happiness could have taken form in these words: 'Thank God, thank God that I am like other men, that I am only a man among

15

others.' . . . I have the immense joy of being a man, a member of a race in which God himself became incarnate . . . And if only everybody could realise this! But it cannot be explained. There is no way of telling people that they are all walking around shining like the sun![10]

Such 'moments of transcendence', which take people beyond the narrow confines of the individual self, are deeply part of being human, and though we may not have experienced them in the vivid ways described here, few of us have not at least glimpsed them.

Such glimpses might have come at moments of intense intimacy with a loved one; or moments of overwhelming gratitude in a church, temple or holy place; or drinking in a scene of great natural beauty; or listening to music; or gazing at a great work of art or architecture. Paradoxically, it might have been a moment when we realised we were carrying a heavy burden of pain or hurt in our lives. We found, despite its awfulness, that we were able to 'own' that pain or grief, perhaps through the help of others close to us. And we found that as we were able to integrate the loss or pain into our experience, strangely we discovered a new 'at-one-ness' both within ourselves, and with others through a kind of shared vulnerability.

Or such moments might be through very ordinary everyday experiences which, nevertheless, we find somehow glorious. It might be creating or building something worthwhile and beautiful with others. Or as in the case of Thomas Merton, it may simply be a moment of standing in a shopping precinct, really seeing people in all their uniqueness and loveliness, with an overwhelming sense of delight – almost as though it were for the first time.

These are the moments in our lives when we sense most deeply what human life is about. A religious dimension is inescapably part and parcel of them as we become aware, even if only for a fleeting moment, that our life is tinged with a Mystery that somehow surrounds us and is even deeply within us. Such moments point to a unitive vision of existence in which we experience ourselves not as isolated individuals but as part of something infinitely bigger. Such moments can be hugely important in our lives even though we may not understand precisely what is happening to us. They give hope to the idea of belief, and they lead to the question: Is there another way of praying that is less to do with words and more to do with learning a kind of deeper 'receptivity'?

At this point it may be said: Is this not simply to affirm what has always been taught in the Christian tradition – that God is the ground of all life, and in him 'we live and move and have our being'? The most basic truth of faith is that God is indeed the ground of all life. But the trouble is we do not seem to know it in our experience. Somehow, it remains largely hidden from us. And for much of the time, our experience of daily life suggests entirely the opposite.

Multiple overwhelmings

For regular churchgoers as much as anyone else, much of life feels a long way away from any living sense of the Mystery of God. Rather than having experiences of grace and wonder, people speak of just surviving the pressures of the modern world; what one writer has called 'the multiple overwhelmings' that are faced at an ever-increasing pace. Or people feel besieged by all kinds of powerful and negative forces within them, forces that they do not always fully understand and which sometimes do indeed overwhelm – persistent anxiety, profound and sometimes inexplicable feelings of guilt, painful fears, burning resentments, aching griefs.

Or people find that modern life is just so demanding, noisy and distracting that it would seem impossible ever to be able to find the time and space needed to gain any sustained sense of the Mystery of God – even if we knew how to seek it.

And so for these reasons also, even I suspect for church people, praying remains remote. We feel we ought to do it, but somehow its vitality eludes us. And sadly our experience of the church so often leads us to go on thinking of it as being to do with a lot of formal and lifeless words, usually uttered by religious professionals.

The need to pray

However, despite all of this, the need to pray does not just vanish. Despite the underminings of doubt and the overwhelmings of life, people find that somehow they don't want to give up.

The thirst for an authentic spirituality simply persists. The history of the human race would suggest that humankind is inescapably religious.

However outwardly content or materially secure life may become, people go on experiencing a kind of void within that will not be easily shrugged off, an emptiness and need that won't disappear. And it is a perplexing truth that the more affluent and secure life becomes, the more that inner hunger seems to grow. Sometimes we intuitively know that whatever doubts there may be about God in the mind, this need within can only be truly met and satisfied by some kind of experience of the heart, of the spirit. And so, even though our culture is now far adrift from the traditions, customs and rituals that sustained our ancestors, the search for authentic spirituality continues, even if at times people scarcely know what it is that they are looking for.

St Augustine said that God has made us for himself and, specifically, 'Our hearts are restless until they find their rest in thee'.

This quotation lives on and is repeated again and again in the life of the Church, perhaps because at a profound and intuitive rather than a rational level, people somehow know what the words mean. Perhaps enough has been glimpsed of the power of authentic spirituality in other people's lives to recognise the truth of them. And these words challenge us to think about prayer more deeply, and not to give up the search for it. If we are to have any hope of finding out just what they mean – in experience and not just theory – then somehow we must go on trying to pray.

But how do we do it? What does it involve? How can it be sustained?

At this point it is important to acknowledge the seeming impossibility, even the absurdity of this project, the extraordinary nature of its suggestion. Can it really be possible for human beings in the midst of the struggles and contingencies of our lives . . . in the midst of our smallness and frailty and complexity and mortality . . . to become one with the Mystery of the Origin of Life? This is the extraordinary claim of religious faith. How can it possibly be?

By way of some kind of answer, it is worth pointing in two directions: Firstly, to the creative power of artists, writers, poets and musicians who offer sometimes breathtaking glimpses of beauty; and secondly to the path walked by those who have selflessly given their lives in the service of others. Wherever beauty or sacrifice are seen we recognise the transcendent shining through, transforming and lighting up the world around. Beauty in art, and compassion, vulnerability and self-giving risk in people; these are the tell-tale marks of the presence of the Mystery of the Divine. And so we may say that there is a sense in which prayer, understood as the glimpsing of the Divine shining in and through humans, is 'happening' all the time around us, amongst us, even within us. But do we have the eyes to see it? And what are the clues as to how we too may enter into that which is both gloriously present, and yet also mysteriously elusive and hidden?

That is the problem; seeing and believing in the Mystery of Love which is all around us – what the poet Gerard Manley Hopkins called 'the grandeur of God' with which the world is 'charged'[11] – and yet is at the same time strangely hidden from us. This 'seeing' does not just happen. Such is the extent of our blindness, our noisiness, and our alienation, that to see the vision of that glory involves a long and arduous journey on which again and again, only fleeting glimpses are given. But the vision – and the journey – is what we are made for. One of the early Fathers, St Basil of Caesarea, wrote: 'The human being is an animal who has received the vocation to become God.'[12] It is an extraordinary statement, implying not only 'seeing' but also becoming one with the glory. 'The glory of God,' wrote Irenaeus, 'is a living person and the life of humanity is the vision of God.'[13] Pursuing this vision is the challenge that should question and shape every activity of our lives.

This journey is what the work of prayer is about. The challenge is to prepare and focus the heart so that God may be seen in every situation. It is an activity that is paradoxically not an 'activity' at all, and it must be entered into both with others, and alone.

It is with the task of structuring time alone that this introduction and guide is concerned. It is an attempt to help the modern pilgrim find his or her own way to a more authentic life of personal prayer, to explore how each of us may interpret the advice given in the tradition of the Desert Fathers by the revered Abba Moses. When a brother came to him and begged for a word, he replied, 'Go and sit in your cell and your cell will teach you everything.' What does that seemingly bleak recipe mean for us? How can modern human beings of the western world face up to the daunting questions of silence and solitude implied in it?

A practical manual

The Guide (pp. 54-171) adopts an essentially practical approach. There are many valuable books which explore in greater or lesser depth different approaches to prayer and tell the story of the long tradition of prayer; but too often the literature leaves readers saying to themselves, 'That is all very well, but how on earth do I begin – and how do I go on?'

I hope that what is offered here will address some of the questions of 'how' without becoming too simplistic, or implying that there is a fixed and clear and prescribed way that magically 'works'. Prayer is always a struggle and each of us has to find our own way. But I hope that what is written here will provide a guide for the ordinary church member or anyone interested in the quest for a spiritual life, who feels the need for something simple and practical to get them under way. Or it may be helpful to those who already have an established way of prayer as they explore further their experience of God. But it is limited in scope. It does not attempt to answer all the questions, and it is certainly not a kind of total prescription. It is simply a practical manual for the exciting task of actually beginning. I hope that readers, whatever their experience, will make it their own by flexibly adapting what is offered.

Learning from and with others

Two final points:

Firstly, always remember that in this business of praying, there are no experts. Everyone is different and everyone is always learning. People's experience of prayer develops and grows in different ways. However there is a long tradition of contemplative prayer to draw upon, to which the Guide makes reference all the way through – the experience of women and men of prayer down the centuries that can help us, as we stumblingly learn too. These glimpses into the experience of others who have been deeply immersed in the tradition will be found in the plain boxes printed at the bottom of the right-hand page each week. They are there to encourage. In the shaded boxes above there is a different kind of encouragement: a reflection on the actual experience of praying. It aims to encourage the reader with the demanding challenge of the task and alludes to some of the obstacles that may be encountered. Often the content of these two 'boxes' will reflect a theme from the Gospel passage for the week.

Secondly, although the focus in this guide is on time spent alone, from time to time it is helpful to meet and share experiences with others in a group. If you are part of a Church or Christian community look for opportunities to explore this area with others. See if some kind of meeting can be arranged where a pooling of experience can take place and some silence can be shared. Thus there can be a mutual strengthening in the face of this huge challenge which, though it must be pursued in solitude, does not lead into aloneness but into an extraordinary and all-pervading at-one-ness – a uniting – with oneself, with others, and with the Mysterious Ground of all life.

CHAPTER 2 WHAT DO I NEED? FOUR ESSENTIALS

The substance of the Guide consists of a simple weekly/daily outline suggesting how your time might be used. However, before we get into this it is important to ask whether there are any essential preconditions.

Think of the analogy of trying to grow plants. Every gardener knows that there are certain preconditions to growing a healthy plant. If you chuck a few seeds out onto some rough weed-strewn wasteland, without any attempt to dig the ground, clear the weeds, and ensure adequate light, warmth and moisture, it will be no great surprise when nothing comes up!

It is the same with praying. If the tender plant of the life of prayer is to have any chance of taking root and growing in a person, four basic conditions are essential:

- time
- space
- solitude
- silence

Time

First, a discipline of setting aside specific time is essential. While prayer means a struggle to see all life and every moment under God – so it cannot be limited to specific times – it nevertheless needs specific times. Unless we set aside a particular time, nothing will happen.

Second, as well as specific times, it needs a long time, even a lifetime. Prayer is about change. It is a mysterious process of human transformation through the grace of God, but it is gradual and gentle, like a plant growing. Nothing is going to happen overnight.

As you set out there are three obvious questions:

- how frequently should I pray?
- at what time of day?
- for how long?

It is important to be realistic. If you are going to establish a new habit of life, you need a rule that has some chance of being followed and that will survive the pressures of your work, family and household and what you understand of your own personality. As you think ahead and begin to work something out, be gentle with yourself and think carefully. Try to aim for a goal that you think has some chance of success.

Let's look at the three time questions in more detail:

How frequently should I pray?
Those who write about praying and publish prayer notes normally assume a daily pattern of praying. It is best if you can do that, and worth aiming for. However, a daily pattern may be a huge jump from where you are now. It may be more realistic to think at first in terms of a weekly pattern or perhaps twice weekly. Most people have one or two days in the week, normally the weekend, which are less pressured and which offer a greater chance of empty time.

Think carefully about creating these spaces in your week, and when you have decided, put them in the diary and look forward to them. See them as times that nothing will move you from, although there will be many pressures against you. Realise at the outset that you are aiming to do something that will be considered by most people in our culture as odd. And all of us have internalised the attitudes of the society around us, so as you sit down to pray it will be surprising if you do not feel this is odd too. Going to church regularly is one thing, but setting aside time to pray . . . and on your own? Much will discourage you, including perhaps even other members of your household. You may well feel these pressures quite personally, so it is as well to be prepared before you start. Remember the story Jesus of Nazareth told about the king who set off to do battle but did not reckon on the cost of the enterprise.

And then be prepared for the inevitable discouragement when the whole project seems to be failing. You are probably embarking on something quite new, which will challenge deeply ingrained habits and patterns in your personality. It is something that is both simple and difficult. Initially you may well be excited and full of anticipation as you embark on what is a potentially life-transforming quest. The first experiences of more prolonged silence and focused adoration may be charged with wonder and a sense of mystery, or you may find an extraordinary and unbelievable peacefulness surrounding you as you begin to enter into your practice.

But be prepared as you hit the wall of nothingness and emptiness and feel plagued by distractions, and begin to wonder if you are falling into a kind of futile daydreaming. Abba Moses said go and sit in your cell, and your cell – nothing else – will teach you everything. As you set out to be open to another unseen and hidden world there are no words to read, no music to hear, no TV to watch, no radio to listen to. It is a world that challenges all the nostrums of the culture we live in; a world of silence, stillness, emptiness, waiting. It is a world of believing but not knowing, in which we struggle to leave behind our minds, most particularly our minds, as we wait and hope for the God who reveals himself in the silence of the heart.

Keeping to and persevering with what Jesus called this 'narrow way' is not easy. Many times you will feel like giving up, and maybe you will indeed give up for long periods. Weeks may go by without finding time to pray. If that happens try not to feel guilty and do not despair. Remember that something new is slowly being born in you that can take a long time to become established. And even if you do find your practice is slow and intermittent don't be discouraged.

Over the months as you persist, you will slowly acquire a taste for this strange activity as you begin to glimpse now and again the experience of something that is both mysteriously beyond you, and also deeply within you. You will find that you are beginning to tread upon a deeper and more secure 'ground' within yourself that is somehow given in and through the practice of your silence. And this taste for prayer will not easily leave you. Although persistent attention is required, and a gritty determination to go to your place alone needs to be summoned time and again, you will slowly become aware that it is not just a matter of discipline and will. You begin to find that something deeper, lovelier and more long-lasting than mere disciplined persistence is beginning to happen within you – you are being gently drawn into an affair of the heart. You are discovering from your own experience that we human beings have a need written deeply in our nature to respond to the first commandment: to love God with heart, mind, soul and strength. That, it would seem, is the way we are made. We are beginning to find that seeking God is not just a religious duty but – gloriously – the fulfilment of who we most fundamentally are.

So we gradually discover a new appetite being born in us. We need this praying, and though it remains difficult, we know we must seek this praying. Although it is certainly going against the grain of the world around we begin to discover that it is actually to go *with* the deepest grain of what it means to be human. It becomes a matter of necessity as we slowly attune ourselves to something that is already there within, what one writer has likened to a kind of hidden music that we may have forgotten the sound of, but is still there, still playing.

Responding to that inner music takes us eventually beyond the disciplines of time. Will and discipline are certainly needed, but we eventually find that it is not just to do with the will, but a matter of what we most deeply want. In theological language, it is a matter of 'grace'. We find we are being gently drawn by the Spirit of God into the depths of God.

What time of day?
People respond differently to the times of the day, but early morning is usually the best time, when the world is quiet and before the demands of the day are upon us.

Our days are a microcosm of our lives. Each morning is potentially a kind of new birth – a new beginning. In the night we have descended into the strange world of the subconscious – into hidden layers of memories and dreams and strange connections. Before we meet the demands of the day ahead we need to 'come to' and be silent and still, to allow ourselves to emerge from the night, and find ourselves again as we focus on something deeper than dreams.

In the early morning we are also less likely to be tired, and so more able to sustain the kind of focused attention that is needed.

For how long?
Overall, it is important to have modest aims, particularly at the beginning.

This avoids feelings of failure when you find initially that you are not able, or simply do not wish to pray for very long. Length of time will depend on how you structure your time.

In this guide, a threefold structure of *Stilling, Offering,* and *Reflecting* is suggested and explored in Chapter 3: 'What do I do? Shaping the time'. All three have their place, but the crucial ingredient of any time of prayer is the first – learning how to be still and focused. It is in this essential work that the difficult task of leaving behind the activity and distractions of the thinking mind takes place; it is here that the door can open into the unfamiliar world of the heart's silent and attentive waiting. So don't neglect it, it is the key.

At first try five or ten minutes as you practise the unfamiliar discipline of stillness and focusing. As you get accustomed to it, try lengthening your time to fifteen or twenty minutes, or even half an hour.

Following the time of Stilling, which involves a journey inward to the point where you become 'grounded' in the adoration of the heart, the time of Offering involves a journey outwards again as you look ahead to the events, encounters and tasks of the day ahead, and the challenges you face. But it need not be long; God knows what our needs are. Lists of names or mentioning the details of concerns are not necessary. The time of Offering is there so that, grounded in the adoration of God, we may hold to our inner life in the face of what is to come and see with the eyes of compassion and hope the people and concerns that lie before us.

The third part – Reflecting – is best done at another time of the day as it involves an engagement of the mind, and therefore to some extent 'conflicts' with the emphasis in the first part. However, it is a most important part of the practice of Christian contemplative prayer and will require a focused period of time if you are really going to dig into the meanings in the Gospel. As with the period of Stilling begin gently – five minutes at first, growing to ten or fifteen or longer as you develop the practice of reading the Gospel in a distinctively contemplative way.

In terms of your time all three are important, though learning to be still at the beginning of any prayer time is the most important. If you do nothing else in your week, beginning to be still and sitting in the healing silence of God will be sufficient.

The discipline of sticking to a fixed length of time whatever feelings may come is good, but don't get hung up on time. Be flexible and gentle with yourself. Remember it is not ultimately you who are doing the praying. With discipline and perseverance, you are seeking to be open, focused and receptive, allowing time for the Spirit of God to find you, love you, pray in you, and take you into worship.

Space

Where are you going to do this praying thing? As well as a specific period of time, you will need a place – some corner of a room, or an attic or basement, perhaps just a particular chair or cushion in a quiet bedroom; somewhere where you can go alone where you will be entirely undisturbed, away from even the caring presence of those close to you.

Jesus said, 'Go into your room and pray to your Father in secret . . .' A 'secret' or private place is needed. In her book *Motherhood and God*, Margaret Hebblethwaite writes of how when she was a young mother, besieged by the needs of three small children, she made her own prayer place in an under-stairs cupboard in the basement of her home. She carpeted it, arranged the lighting, and decorated it with postcards and pictures of her family as well as symbols of the Love of God – a crucifix, and the face of the Turin Shroud. She writes:

> When I sit in this little, low prayer place, facing the crucifix and the Shroud face, with the lighted candle below them and a narrow shaft of light from the grating slanting down from above, then I feel a great sense of spaciousness. Around may be the noises of the house – the children running in and out of the garden and sending shadows over the grating as they do so . . . the washing machine, humming and glugging through the floor a few feet above my right shoulder . . . the neighbours who for some reason can be heard more clearly here than through any other section of the party wall. But I feel I am resting here in the centre of things, in the hidden centre of my home, in the secret centre of my soul, and that centre is a place of calm and light and space.[14]

Later she adds:

> I need my prayer hole because I am bad at praying. I need it because I
> can just go in and do nothing and then I am praying. It takes the effort
> out of it, and the dread, and the fear of boredom, and the distractions.
> It cuts down the interruptions too: when I am in my prayer hole people
> do not burst in on me. If they need me they call respectfully. They do
> not break in on that fragile, vulnerable core of being that we need to let
> unfold gently in the sight of God.

Space matters. As well as churches, which are holy spaces in communities, we
need holy spaces at home where we may, 'unfold gently in the sight of God'.

Solitude

This may be the biggest challenge. The faith journey is in essence a
community venture. We are baptised into the Body of Christ, and need to
share regularly in the Eucharist. The Christian faith *is* life in community.
We discover that life with others and through others as we listen, receive,
share, serve, contribute and belong. We *need* to belong, for we are
members one of another and our love for God is expressed and found in and
through our love for one another. Christianity is never a religion of private
experience. This corporate emphasis is fundamental.

But there is another emphasis – we also need to be alone. It is the forgotten
part of the journey and, in the contemporary church, teaching about the
practice of it has been seriously neglected.

We need both emphases. The journey in community, the shared life and
liturgy of the Church, saves praying from becoming too personally focused.
It reminds us of the huge narrative of the tradition of which we are a part,
of the wider body of which we are a member. The liturgy nourishes, teaches
and forms us, and by our participation in it we help to build up and
encourage others as we become the Body of Christ, discovering Christ
among us. But the journey alone is crucial too, and intimately related to the
life in community. On that journey we find we have a self to offer to others,
and a self where we meet others. Thomas Merton wrote: 'The more we are
alone with God, the more we are with one another.'[15] We find that our

solitary practice deepens and enriches a sense of profound belonging to others, and nourishes the life of public prayer, helping to prevent it from becoming dull, dead or merely formal.

In the tradition of contemplative spirituality, solitude has always been recognised as essential. If we are ever going to discover who we really are and to learn what it means to love our neighbour as we love ourselves, we must pursue it. Unless at some point you hide, even from the loving gaze of others, you will never finally know who you are. Such is the essential privacy and mystery of our being.

In one of his essays on the contemplative experience, Thomas Merton likens the soul, or inner self, to 'a very shy wild animal that never appears at all whenever an alien presence is at hand, and comes out only when all is peaceful, in silence, when he is untroubled and alone.'[16]

Without solitude the Church becomes a happy herd of the like-minded: noisy, banal and superficial. But solitude is not easy. We have to learn to be alone.

Silence

Finally, we need silence. Silence in the Christian and monastic tradition is far more than the absence of noise. It has been called 'the first language of God'. Silence more than anything else takes us into the Mystery itself. So although times of prayer may include words and music, it is above all an adventure in silence.

However, like being alone, being silent also goes against the grain, and may be something that is quite hard to keep to in many households. From the moment we wake in the morning and turn on the radio, to the last moment of the day when the TV is turned off we surround ourselves with incessant noise. There is a need to fill the blank and even threatening emptiness that silence would suggest. So there can be a deep resistance to silence and at first we do have to 'force ourselves' into it. However, if we stay with it we find that it brings huge rewards – sometimes what feels like a kind of breakthrough to another dimension of being.

Here's an account from the writings of a fourth-century Syrian monk, Isaac of Nineveh, recorded in Thomas Merton's book *Contemplative Prayer*:

Many are avidly seeking, but they alone find who remain in continual silence . . . Every man who delights in a multitude of words, even though he says admirable things, is empty within. If you love truth, be a lover of silence. Silence like the sunlight will illuminate you in God and will deliver you from the phantoms of ignorance. Silence will unite you to God himself . . .

More than all things love silence; it brings you a fruit that tongue cannot describe. In the beginning we have to force ourselves to be silent. But then there is born something that draws us to silence. May God give you an experience of this 'something' that is born of silence. If only you practise this, untold light will dawn on you in consequence . . . after a while a certain sweetness is born in the heart of this exercise and the body is drawn almost by force to remain in silence.[17]

CHAPTER 3 WHAT DO I DO? SHAPING THE TIME

You have decided to set aside time each week, or even each day. Your first prayer time arrives. You go into your room. You shut the door. You are alone. It is silent. You experience bewilderment – what are you going to do?

Think of the time of prayer in three stages:

- time for Stilling and Centring
- time for Offering
- time for Reflecting

We will explore each in turn.

Stilling and Centring

Becoming still in body and mind takes us to the very heart of what prayer is about.

Praying is:

- A commitment to turn from the multitude of concerns at the fore-front of the mind towards the Mystery of Christ, and in the words of the Gospel of John, to seek to 'abide in him'. It is a commitment to live out again and again the promise of Baptism: 'I turn to Christ.'

- A discovery – in experience – of the meaning of the opening words of Jesus in the Gospel of Matthew: 'Repent (to 'turn'), for the Kingdom of Heaven is at hand.' But, as he made clear throughout his Gospel, the Kingdom which is 'at hand' is nevertheless not immediately appar-ent. It is a treasure completely hidden. It can be most disconcerting. As you sit down and seek to be still, nothing at first seems to be there.

- A process whereby we slowly begin to sense within us the truth of Psalm 46: 'Be still and know that I am God . . .' The words suggest we shall not 'know' this extraordinary experience of 'being itself', within and beyond us, unless we are 'still'. But learning to be still takes a long time, even a lifetime. Patience and persistence are essential.

It is not easy, and it will continue not to be easy. A strong intention of the heart and the discipline of a rule are needed; but also faith. Christ *is* with us; the Kingdom will appear.

How to begin? Think of it in two stages: Preparation and Focusing.

Preparation

Archbishop Michael Ramsey was once asked: 'How long have you prayed today, Archbishop?' After a pause he said, 'About a minute, but it took me twenty-nine to get there.'

Our minds are scattered and distracted. Sometimes we are quite deeply alienated – 'out of sorts' – with others and ourselves. It takes time to come to, begin to turn round, and set out on the long journey home. As you set out it is best to begin with your body.

Below are suggestions to help you prepare to find your way to the borders of prayer.

Find a comfortable position sitting on a chair, or sitting cross-legged on a cushion on the floor. Or use a 'prayer stool' (a simple wooden support that goes over the ankles enabling you to sit back in a kneeling position). Find the position that best suits you. The main thing is to be comfortable and yet alert.

Sit still with your back straight and head up. Relax the muscles around your shoulders. Let your hands be cupped in your lap, or resting on your knees, palms up or down.

Gently close your eyes. This helps to focus your attention. However, some people like to place a visual focus in front of them, perhaps a lit candle, or an icon.

Relax the body and deepen the breathing. Try focusing for a few moments on the breath going in and out as you slowly fill and empty your lungs. You can connect breathing with the Spirit of God – it is the same word, 'ruach' in Hebrew. Breathe the Spirit into every part of you. Don't rush. Enjoy your sitting and beginning to be still. And as you sit, be aware of the silence around you.

As part of preparation, some people find it helpful to spend time going further into relaxing and centring through some simple stretching exercises. This can be a very helpful way of deepening stillness of body and mind.

Focusing

As you begin to breathe steadily and be still, you are likely to become acutely aware of sounds and distractions around you . . . a door creaking, a fly buzzing, traffic outside, other people in the house, the ticking of a clock, your tummy rumbling. You begin to discover that you are in a state of heightened mental alertness, picking up sounds that in the normal course of life would go by unnoticed. Don't let them bother you. Simply identify what they are – and then leave them be.

And then as you sit, ignoring outward distractions, you begin to find that the noise is more inside than out. However much you may wish to be still, the mind is not nearly as biddable as the body. In the silence you are bombarded by a disconcerting array of thoughts, impressions, memories, concerns, arguments, fantasies, and anxieties. This mental cacophony comes welling up without invitation and can be extremely difficult to control. As we try to concentrate, we are beginning to face the daunting challenge of this way of prayer. We are beginning to enter into the heart of the matter.

This path of contemplative prayer involves seeking a kind of breakthrough from the habitual world of rational activity – of thinking, assessing, clarifying, evaluating, judging, asserting, calculating, planning, etc., into a realm that is both within us but is also mysteriously beyond us. It is certainly beyond the sphere of our rational minds in terms of how they normally work, but this is not to dismiss the rational functioning of the mind. In order to live and deal effectively with the world around, we need the clarifying, assessing, and thinking activity of the brain. And in terms of our faith we need it for the task of theological learning and exploration so that we can gain a measure of understanding of just what it is that we believe.

But – and it is a crucial 'but' that the Church has largely forgotten – the mystical tradition starkly tells us that God cannot be reached by the activity of thought itself. 'By love he can be caught and held,' wrote the anonymous author of *The Cloud of Unknowing*, 'but by thinking never.'[18] And so quite simply we have to commit ourselves, by an act of determined, repeated and constant attention, to the difficult task of laying our 'thinking' minds aside. The challenge is to find a way of stilling the ceaseless chatter of the brain so that slowly we pass into another realm where rational activity and categorisation gradually cease. It is a more 'inner' state, more centred and more unified, a deeper realm of the spirit, where we may slowly discover a profound and healing sense of 'at-one-ness'. We begin to sense that here we somehow deeply belong.

This strange kind of inner 'passover' journey needs to be undertaken again and again. It is a pilgrimage of the soul that must be constantly repeated, a movement from our self-centred preoccupations and anxieties, and constant tendency to self-justification, into the Mystery of the Other, of Christ, of God.

'I turn to Christ'. It is easy to say but how does one begin to accomplish it? What help does the long tradition of contemplative prayer offer, so that this turning, this pilgrimage of the soul, may be made?

The tradition tells us that we need a simple focus that will hold the attention of the mind, and gently take the one who prays down below the level of the chattering clamouring brain into the silence of the heart, directing us – mind and heart at one – towards the Mystery of God.

Over the centuries, teachers of the contemplative way have recommended choosing just one word or phrase and gently and rhythmically repeating it, in time with the breath.

The focus does not have to be a word. Some find an image helpful, or an icon, a picture, an object, or beads. In the Buddhist tradition, focusing on the breath as it comes in and out of the nose is recommended. However, most people in the Christian tradition who begin this way of praying use a prayer phrase, which becomes a focus for the mind and an anchor for the heart.

The purpose is to do what seems initially impossible – to cease from all discursive rational activity, all 'thinking' – and so to enter into the 'heart' which is the centre and core of the affections. Thus the whole person gradually becomes engaged in an act of focused adoration. In the Hindu tradition it is called becoming 'one-pointed'. In the Christian tradition it may be likened to the practice of Mary of Bethany who sat at the feet of Jesus choosing 'the one thing necessary'.

Through the development of this practice we slowly – and with a kind of painstaking deliberateness – clear an inner space where we may silently worship the One who is beyond us and yet also within us. As we patiently persist in this practice, we may eventually reach a point where our focus, our word or phrase or whatever else we use, becomes redundant. It is a point where the noise of the mind finally ceases, and we find we have entered into such a profound stillness that we may no longer even be aware of ourselves praying.

This 'method' of contemplative prayer is very ancient and has parallels in the other great faiths. In the Christian tradition it can particularly be traced from the experience of the Desert Fathers of ancient Egypt. In recent years the teaching of it has been revived, particularly through the writings of a Benedictine monk, Fr John Main, who in the early 1970s founded a world-wide network to support individuals and groups in the practice of this form of prayer. Others, notably the American monk Thomas Merton, who died in 1968, and Fr Bede Griffiths, who died in India in 1993, have pointed towards it through their writings and so have encouraged more and more people to persevere in finding the contemplative path.

Which focus?

There are many, of course. However, the main focus of attention here is the use of either a phrase from the Psalms, or one word or name. But we shall also touch briefly on alternative approaches.

1. The Psalms

One or two phrases from a psalm, which will be printed in the notes each week can serve as a good initial focus. The Psalms were the daily bread of prayer for Jesus himself. Much of the shape and form of the words that have come down to us grew originally out of their use in the prayer and worship of synagogue and temple. They are often repetitive in style leading worshippers deeper and deeper into the Mystery of God and they are extraordinarily expressive of the longings and needs of the heart. By their use of imagery, and their intimate directness, they offer a rich vocabulary that can take the praying person into the heart of adoration.

However, they are long and brimming with words. What is needed is just a few words that will open the way to a place of no words. Therefore each week one phrase is suggested to simply act as an anchor and focus. As people begin to pray in this way, they find that they get attached to a few particular phrases which help them and to which they return again and again.

I find the opening words of Psalm 18 powerful and consoling:

> 'I love you, O Lord, my strength; O Lord, my crag, my fortress and my deliverer.'

Or the first line of Psalm 63 which centres the individual very personally in God in the first part, and then directs one beyond oneself towards God in the second part, indicating that we both know him and don't know him:

> 'O God, you are my God, eagerly will I seek you.'

The first line of Psalm 42 offers a beautiful image which powerfully evokes the depth of human need:

> 'As the deer longs for the water-brooks, so longs my soul for you, O God; my soul is athirst for God, athirst for the Living God.'

The words of Psalm 84, verse 5, with their sense of journeying, convey a positive and robust feel with this metaphor of 'highways' in the heart:

> 'Blessed is the one whose strength is in you, in whose heart are the highways to Zion.'

('Zion' meaning the place of God's dwelling).

All these phrases speak of a hunger and longing for God and a living forwards into God. When repeated in focused adoration, they can lead the worshipper into a depth of devotion that may surprise them. During the day the phrase can be visited again, and can go on echoing in the mind, stilling, centring, focusing, and directing.

The power of the imagination. When using a phrase in this way, don't be afraid to use the imagination. The images are powerfully evocative. For example the words 'My crag, my fortress and my deliverer' speak of profound longings for safety, protection and freedom which exist in all of us. For everyone these words will have powerful resonances connecting us with some of our most fundamental needs as human beings. They may evoke quite specific instances or places when we knew just what it meant to be safe, protected, or free. We know beyond rational knowledge what these words mean, their truths are hidden in us. We need to stay with the meanings we find and allow them to resonate within us – they are of God.

But there is another way that is even simpler.

2. One phrase or word
A variation of this approach is always to use just one phrase or word, and keep to it.

Gently and constantly repeated, the one phrase or word becomes a kind of bedrock in the depths of the individual's mind – like an eastern mantra. As it is silently repeated again and again, it goes deeper and deeper into the mind and so to the heart and core of the person, until it becomes so familiar and so embedded that it even feels as though it becomes a part of them. For this reason it is important to stick to the same phrase or word and not to change it. At first it may feel very strange but after some time of this practice the individual may find that the phrase they have chosen, and which has become more and more part of them, begins gently, even involuntarily, to sound within them when they are out and about in their everyday lives doing other things.

For Christians, there is a strong tradition of using the name of Jesus Christ himself, or alternatively the intimate name of God that Jesus used, which was such a new teaching in his day and which he taught and encouraged his disciples to use and to 'hallow' – *Abba, Father.*

(It is worth adding that this repetition of the holy name of God is a powerful tradition in other religions also. In Hinduism, the repetition of the name of God is a Yoga – called 'Japa Yoga' – and regarded as one of many ways of achieving union with the Divine; and in Sufism, the mystical tradition within Islam, it is called the practice of the 'dhikr', the repetition of a sacred word or one of the ninety-nine sacred names of God.)

For many Christians, the 'Jesus Prayer' which is so loved in the Eastern Orthodox tradition and which consists of the simple and constant repetition of the name of Christ offers the ideal form for this kind of praying. The complete version is *'Lord Jesus Christ, Son of God, have mercy on me'.* When prayed over and over again it can have the effect of entirely capturing the heart of the one who prays. This was the 'mantra' which the Benedictine Fr Bede Griffiths said was the basis of his praying life. However, for some it may be too long. If so, it can be shortened to *'Lord Jesus Christ, Son of God'* or *'Lord Jesus Christ, have mercy on me'*, repeated in time with the breathing. Or try simply using the name of Christ alone: *'Lord Jesus Christ' – Lord* on the in-breath, *Jesus Christ* on the out-breath, pausing for a moment on the word *Christ* at the end.

This rhythm of breathing can be the same with *'Abba, Father'.*

Writing of this practice in his book *This Sunrise of Wonder*, Michael Mayne says:

> Words that I love to use are from that verse from the hymn known as St Patrick's Breastplate which begins, 'Christ be with me, Christ within me' and ends 'Christ in mouth of friend and stranger.' To say such words slowly, repeatedly, means that they gradually become part of you and may then well up from within you quite outside your formal times of prayer.[19]

The Benedictine Monk Fr John Main, writing on the practice of praying in this way, recommends as a prayer word, or 'Mantra' as he calls it, the use of an Aramaic word which comes at the very end of the New Testament – *Maranatha*. It means *Come Lord (Jesus)*. It is a beautiful, stilling and rhythmic sound, centring the whole person – body, mind and spirit – in God. However, although it does have an extraordinary kind of resonance some may feel that, being from another language, it is just too strange, and doesn't sufficiently connect them with the meaning of adoration in the same way that the name of Christ or God does. Experiment and find what best suits you – and then stick to it.

Two different but similar approaches. These two approaches – the psalms, or the one phrase or name – both require the same focused attention and the gentle repetition of words, but they also differ in important respects. The psalms offer a rich variety of images that speak of human need for divine help. They can be very evocative, and when persisted with can powerfully engage the spiritual imagination.

The second way is more 'one-pointed', and leads to a more total shutting down of the mind, and can take the individual very deeply into the soul.

Allow your own practice to develop as you think best and at your own pace, adding in whatever extra ingredients you find helpful. It is always important to remember that there are no right or wrong answers, there is only the best way for each of us.

On pages 49 and 50 is a summary of the guidelines which apply to the two approaches described above. Adapt them as feels best for you.

Launching into this kind of praying will at first feel odd and perhaps uncomfortable. But as you find your place alone, and set out to be still, remember that no one is watching you, no one is listening! Huge numbers of people have prayed and do pray daily in this way. You are in very good company. Just keep to the simple guidelines, persevere in the face of difficulties, and leave the rest to the love of God.

3. Alternative approaches

After trying this kind of approach, and recognising the need to persist when the novelty has worn off, some people may come to feel that, whilst still wishing to find an essentially contemplative path, they need more material to work with. If the approach outlined here is just too sparse for you, that's fine. We have to be experimenters. As children remind us, it's the only way to learn. There are ways of prayer that while following a contemplative approach, use more material. As a wise person once said: 'Pray as you can and do not try to pray as you can't.'[20]

One prayer – The Lord's Prayer. An obvious development of this approach would be to take one complete prayer rather than simply working with one word or phrase, and slowly repeat the phrases of the prayer one by one, allowing the words as much as possible to penetrate below the 'thinking' mind. The Lord's Prayer is best of all, though there are many other possibilities.

However, be careful as you get into the prayer in this way that the mind does not get quickly overloaded, and you return to interpreting and 'thinking about'. In this kind of praying it is always the resonance of the heart that matters. Patiently dwelling on just one phrase at a time can be very rewarding as we discover that each has huge depths of meaning. In Luke's version of the Prayer (Luke 11:2-4), there are just six phrases:

> *Our Father in heaven;*
> *May your name be held holy;*
> *Your Kingdom come;*
> *Give us each day our daily bread;*
> *Forgive us our sins as we forgive each one who is in debt to us;*
> *Do not put us to the test.*

The great twentieth-century spiritual writer and mystic Simone Weil once wrote: 'The "Our Father" contains all possible petitions . . . it is impossible to say it once through, giving the fullest possible attention to every word without a change, infinitesimal perhaps but real, taking place in the soul.'[21]

Or use other media . . . The focus need not just be upon words. Other media and stimuli can be immensely helpful and reach parts of us that words cannot always touch. Some people might want to construct a prayer time that begins and ends with music, perhaps using choral singing from a great cathedral, or maybe just the simple chants of Taizé.

Or you might consider giving careful, disciplined attention to a religious painting, perhaps reading up about it beforehand and then attending to the colour, light, and form of the representation before you, seeking to see what the artist is expressing through his or her work and how their devotion can kindle yours. There are some excellent books that can help you in this. The contemplation of icons which are not mere paintings, but 'windows into God', have for centuries played a most important part in the spirituality of the Orthodox tradition, and are now becoming increasingly popular in the west. Again there are several excellent books on how to pray with them and through them. All of these are ways that can take us beyond our superficial selves into a deeper realm where, for a moment at least, we 'taste and see' that God is – and that God mysteriously is in us.

And there are approaches that are very near to prayer . . . Finally, there are many other ways of using time that, if they are not prayer as such, are very near to it in that they bring us into the crucial attitude of loving and alert attention beyond ourselves, using our skills and talents to 'see' the truth of things, and to celebrate life.

Art is very near to religion, in that it is also about the struggle to see and to open our eyes to a wider vision of reality which otherwise would remain hidden. Music, poetry, painting, sculpture, dance – all are healing and potent in stilling the agitated mind and taking us out of our limited selves and worlds, as can any activity that gives careful and loving attention to the created world – gardening, bird or butterfly watching, conservation work. All of these potentially restore, heal and integrate the whole person.

Done well, all these things remind us of the human capacity to be committed to something that is infinitely greater than ourselves; to be focused, disciplined and still; and to go further than we thought or dreamed was possible at the outset. These activities heal and restore and awaken in us the possibility of transcendence. They point beyond themselves to a glory, which prayer alone can fully find.

Learn to *be still and know* . . . It is the heart of the matter.

But it is not the end of praying. There is a second phase, the Offering of life.

Offering

While learning to become centred and silent in adoration is the main focus of any prayer time, praying cannot end there. There is a world outside to be engaged with, a world in which we are called to be instruments of justice and peace, alert and attentive to the purposes and presence of God. If we are attentive, he can be present to others through us, healing, uniting, consoling, and saving.

So we need to re-engage.

'Offering' means beginning to move in another direction. So far we have worked at closing down the thinking processes of the mind. Gradually and gently we have found a stillness of soul and a focus for the heart's adoration, seeking to become, as one writer in the mystical tradition put it, 'nothing but gazing'. We have remembered again that which we constantly forget – that in the Love of God we are eternally 'found'. But we cannot stay in this place of stillness. We need to move out. The time of offering moves us into the needs and concerns of the day ahead.

It is important to remember here that the task is to foster a contemplative approach. Although we may be taken into a time of intercession for others, we are not primarily talking about 'intercession'. That can happen at other times. Proceeding from our contemplative silence it is more a re-visioning, and re-imaging of the world and ourselves within it, as we are meant to be, and as it is meant to be. Like the blind man at the roadside, our plea is to see again. And seeing again, we can be a light for others. Having been still before this Mystery of Love and discovered again something of its life within us, our concern is simply to offer ourselves in the day ahead, in the encounters and relationships we face and the projects we are engaged with.

As you turn to 'offering' be careful not to get dragged into anxieties. For that reason your time of 'offering' should be brief. It may be helped by some kind of simple symbolic gesture which could become part of your ritual; perhaps no more than the turning of your palms upwards as a sign of 'offering'; or the opening of the pages of the day's diary in front of you. Some simple action or small movement may simply say that your praying is now moving towards its end and towards the world which God loves.

Remember to be very simple. Your silent prayer is that God will simply be God in you and through you; that you will see the world and the people you meet as he sees them, with mercy and love and compassion. You simply wish to be a channel of the freedom of the One who lives in you and those whom you will meet. In the words of the final prayer of the Anglican Eucharist, you simply wish to be 'a living sacrifice', called to action, to make the secular world what it really is – beautiful, sacred, and holy.

And so the prayer time ends; we get up and go.

There is, however, one further dimension that should not be forgotten even if it is only done once during the week – and that is Reflecting.

Reflecting

'Reflecting' simply means allowing the word of the Gospel to penetrate the good soil of a steady heart, to become rooted there, and to grow, shaping and redirecting the whole life of the person.

If our spiritual lives are not to become shapeless or unbalanced we need regularly to read the Gospel – and not just read it, but read it deeply with what St Augustine called 'the eye of the heart' – that we may go on being formed and shaped by the Mystery of Christ within us.

In any mature practice, it is essential to make time to reflect.

In the Guide, at the foot of each weekly page, the reader will find the reference for the Gospel for that Sunday and the week ahead. However, there is a potential difficulty here over timing. Though Reflecting is very much a part of your prayer time, and is still a 'contemplative' activity, it nevertheless demands a more active engagement of the mind, and therefore is probably best done at a different time of the day or week.

To engage in this process of reflection, find a time when you can be alone, quiet and uninterrupted. Spend a few moments centring and being still, and then read the set passage slowly, and at least twice.

Allow time for the text to 'speak'. Don't rush at it and assume that you 'know' or immediately 'understand' what is written – remember there is always more there than you think. Give the passage and yourself time. The brief notes printed at the foot of the page will help by giving a simple summary of the main thrust of the passage and they may open up helpful directions for your reflection that you could usefully explore, but in themselves they cannot tell you how the passage may be a gospel passage for you. So time is needed for your process of discovery. As you sit quietly and read slowly, ask yourself, 'Is there any particular phrase, word, image or scene that catches my attention?' It may be that one word or phrase strikes you, although you don't understand why. If so, stay with that word, repeating it quietly to yourself, seeking out the meanings it has for you that may well be initially elusive to your thinking mind.

Or perhaps as you read, you have an immediate and clear visual image of the scene. Or perhaps there is something about one of the characters that strikes you, although again you may not be quite clear why. Perhaps you intuitively are drawn to, or repelled by one of them. Or perhaps you see yourself in one of them, or identify strongly with a feeling that is being expressed? Without trying too hard, stay with the image, the person, and the scene, attending to what simply comes to you.

Or ask yourself whether there is a particular phrase that is strengthening or seems very direct. If so, gently repeat it several times. If you wish, turn it into a prayer.

The important thing is to develop a kind of receptivity of the heart rather than worrying about understandings. And as you receive insights it may be a good idea to note them down in any personal journal you may keep.

A different kind of reading
Always remember that you are engaged in a contemplative approach, and your reading is part of your praying, even if it is done at a different time. What is important in this part of your prayer, is how you read. It is a contemplative reading of the text, which is not the same as the more familiar practice of 'Bible study' which involves critically thinking 'about' the passage, its authorship, context, purpose, theological ideas, etc., and how it can be

'applied'. A contemplative reading means a different kind of engagement altogether from the familiar, discursive, reasoning kind. Instead of just reading the text, the important thing is to allow the text to explore you.

Remember that although it is describing a scene far away in terms of time and of culture it is nevertheless always about you as a disciple – your need, your response, your discipleship. In the story of the prodigal son, you are the lost son who must leave home. You are also the complaining older brother who doesn't dare to. And within you too there is the sadness and longing, the tears and the huge embrace of acceptance of the welcoming father. He is there also. They are all hidden within you, as is the far country and the pigsty, as well as the home and the long long road to find it.

See the narrative as a narrative of your soul.

To connect with the text in this way, you have to suspend your judgements and your critical faculties and allow the text to speak quite personally and intimately to you. Allow it to dig out the meanings that are already there hidden within you.

It is a way of reading that in the monastic tradition is sometimes called 'Lectio divina' meaning divine or contemplative reading and is quite different to the normal kind of reading. Not so much 'study', it is a kind of attentive and focused listening of the heart, a kind of searching in which one asks, 'How does this passage directly address me, now?'

As with the time of Stilling, it is a matter of faith. We are alone and yet we are not alone. The Mystery of God in some mysterious way seeks to come to us through what we read, to address us, to confront us, to heal us. This does not mean that we become fundamentalists and regard the Bible as infallible from God; nor do we give up on our God-given minds and critical judgements, particularly as to the complex and important questions about the make-up of the New Testament. A critical liberal stance towards the Scriptures is crucial for an intelligent faith. But this is not the time to explore such a stance. A quite different attitude is required, something more silently attentive, more deeply curious, more marked by the crucial quality of ignorance. Not knowing is an absolute prerequisite of finding.

And then having found, or rather having 'been found' again, we go out and live. For that is what the Gospel is about. We read the Gospel not in order that we become more learned or pious, nor so that in some way we can be better at capturing other people for our religion, but simply so that we may be more deeply alive. This is the true aim of all religion – to become transformed into the people that we really are but whom we do not know or have forgotten about. We are created in the image of God and destined for the very likeness of God – nothing less.

For a summary of the guidelines for Reflecting see page 51.

Summary of Stilling and Centring
Using a Phrase from the Psalms

- When you go to your room, sit comfortably either on a chair or on a prayer stool, or cross-legged on a cushion on the floor. Sit with your back straight and head up. If you wish, light a candle or place an icon or some other object in front of you, as a sign of the presence of God. Place your hands gently together on your lap, or on your knees with your palms up or down. Deepen your breathing a little. Be aware of your breath gently filling and emptying your lungs. While remaining alert with back straight let your body relax as you breathe. Be still and remain still. Use any practice you wish to deepen your stillness.

- You may wish to do some gentle stretching exercises, which can deepen stillness. Then return to your seated position. Don't worry if it is not your practice.

- You are alone and yet you are not alone. Believe that, in some mysterious way, God is there – with you, in you.

- Silently in your mind begin to repeat a phrase, or just part of a phrase, from the psalm. Go on repeating it, in time with your breathing if possible. Focus your mind on the meanings that it evokes in you, allowing those meanings to descend from your mind into your 'heart'. Keep gently repeating the phrase, allowing it to be a focus of worship and adoration.

- When your mind wanders off, gently bring it back to the words you are using and keep it focused there. Don't worry if it wanders off again and again. Each time bring it back and focus on the words that you continue to sound in your mind and in your heart, for just as long as you wish.

- If you find that you are led into a deep silence, just allow yourself to be there, in the silence. Finally at the end of the time you may wish to bow gently or even prostrate yourself on the floor. Don't be afraid to use your body.

49

SUMMARY OF STILLING AND CENTRING
USING ONE PHRASE OR NAME

• Sit comfortably with your back straight and head up. Place your hands gently together on your lap, or on your knees, palms up or down. Deepen your breathing a little. Be aware of your breath gently filling and emptying your lungs. While remaining alert with a straight back, let your body relax as you breathe. Be still and remain still. (You may wish to do some gentle stretching exercises, which can deepen stillness. Then return to your seated position.)

• You are alone and yet you are not alone. Believe that, in some mysterious way, God is there – with you, in you.

• Decide on a period of time for this part of your praying. Close your eyes and silently in your mind begin to repeat your prayer phrase or the name you have chosen. Go on repeating it in time with your breathing, if possible. Focus your mind on the phrase or name and nothing else; stick to it through your time, allowing it to descend into your heart. Don't think 'about' the phrase, just focus on it in worship and adoration. Don't think 'about' anything.

• When your mind wanders off, gently bring it back to your prayer phrase and keep it focused there. Don't worry if it wanders off again and again. Each time bring it back and simply focus on the phrase or name, which you continue to sound in your mind, and in your heart.

• Keep gently persevering with it during the time you have set aside. Don't focus on your feelings – look beyond them to the focus of your worship. You are seeking to love God.

• If you find that you are led into a deep silence, just allow yourself to be there, in the silence. Then your word may no longer be necessary. You are simply still in worship and adoration. But if you are distracted by any thoughts, gently come back to the word. Finally at the end of the time, you may wish to bow gently or even prostrate yourself on the floor. Don't be afraid to use your body.

SUMMARY OF GUIDELINES FOR REFLECTING

- Try to decide when is the best time during the week for this part of your praying time. It requires the engagement of the thinking mind to some degree, so it will probably be best to do it at a different time from your normal time of stillness when you are seeking to silence the activity of the brain.

- Read the passage slowly, at least twice.

- Try to listen to the text with your feeling capacity. What is it about? What is happening? What does it suggest? Allow your imagination to work around and get inside different words, phrases or images. How do you engage with it in terms of the needs of your situation, and your heart and soul? Don't rush at it or feel anxious if nothing much seems to come at first. It takes time for meanings to emerge, and so be careful not to assume that you have understood it straightaway. Stay with the meanings that come to you.

- It may well be helpful to take notes which further explore the passage, and how it connects with your situation.

- Find a particular text that 'speaks' to you, or captures your attention, even if you do not quite understand why. Try repeating a word or phrase several times, allowing the text to sink into your heart.

- Be still with what the text has shown you.

- How can you take these meanings and insights into your day?

- Don't worry if there are no insights!

A Guide

for a Year of

Contemplative Prayer

Practical Points for Using the Guide

- The Guide offers an outline for a contemplative approach to prayer covering a whole year, with two pages for each week, and may be used on a daily or weekly basis according to circumstances.

- On the left-hand page the reader is reminded of the three ingredients in this approach to prayer – Stilling, Offering and Reflecting – the main emphasis is on the discipline of stilling the mind and focusing the heart beyond oneself. The reader may soon choose or find their own 'word' or 'mantra' which they will want to keep to. But for each week a verse from the psalms is printed, part of which can act as a phrase for that week or be used in addition or complementary to the reader's own 'word'.

- On the right-hand side are two boxes. The shaded box at the top aims to encourage the reader by offering a reflection on the actual experience of engaging in this kind of praying. This touches on the obstacles that may be encountered, and hints at ways through to the deeper dimension of reality that this kind of prayer is all about. These shaded boxes can simply be read on their own although many of them have grown out of reflection on the Gospel passages and are best read in conjunction with the Gospel.

- The clear box at the bottom contains one or two quotations drawn from a wide variety of sources, and remind us that this way of prayer has been followed by men and women of all faiths over the centuries. They point to the truth that in the loneliness and solitude of this endeavour we are not alone but are surrounded by 'a great cloud of witnesses'.

- The reader will see that the Guide is based on Sundays in the Church's year. This is so that it may be used in any year. However, on the Sundays before Lent that follow the Epiphany season, and on the Sundays that follow Trinity Sunday – and the number of these will differ each year – dates are given at the top of the page. These dates are inclusive. This will guide the reader as to which Sunday it is that the Church is observing – or indeed if that Sunday exists at all in that particular year! At the back of the book on pages 182 and 183, there is a calendar covering the three years from Advent 2000 to the end of 2003 which links the Sundays of the Church's year to the calendar date. Readers would also be helped by buying a copy of the Common Worship Lectionary.

- The Gospel readings that have been chosen for this Guide are from Year C of the Lectionary – the year which focuses mainly on Luke, although as with the other years there are also extracts from John's Gospel. The choice of Luke means that the reader can reflect on some of the best stories in the whole gospel tradition which are only to be found in Luke. In the intervening years these Year C Gospel readings can of course still be used and will offer a contrast with the readings that the reader will hear in the Church's public worship. Alternatively in those other years the reader may simply reflect on the set readings for that year instead of those printed here.

Now – dare to begin!

If you have tried to pray in the past and have given up, I hope that what is offered here may encourage you to begin again. If you already have a discipline of prayer, I hope it will encourage you to continue and go further, adapting and amending what is offered to suit your own pattern. If you have prayed regularly for years, I hope that this Guide will give further encouragement, and will not create any obstacles. However, before we get into it, it is worth repeating a note of caution.

This is a huge adventure, which – if you stick at it – will transform your life. But the challenge of developing a discipline is also very demanding. It requires a dogged persistence, endurance and, as with learning to do anything, practice. At times it will be hard going, and though groups and retreats and conferences are helpful, it will inevitably be mostly solitary. And that is because each of us has to find our own way.

A soul friend or spiritual director is important; a guide such as this may help; the writing and experience of others is hugely valuable; but in the end no one can really teach you. No one can teach you because each of us is unique and our attempts to pray develop in different ways as God the Spirit leads us into the discovery of himself and our own unique selves, created in him. God is the only real teacher. But that is what provides the confidence to begin.

Ultimately prayer is learning to allow God to be God within us. It is an opening to the mysterious action of grace within the soul. God is the beginning and end of it all and, if we let him, he will steadily and gently draw us to himself. See it therefore as an adventure, which may well have small and tentative beginnings, but potentially is the biggest of your life – a journey into the experience of being finally loved and healed.

Dare to begin!

If a not-too-determined Christian were to ask a Zen teacher to teach her to meditate, the conversation might go like this:

Christian	*Sensei, I hear you are skilled in meditation. I am interested in meditation and wonder if we could talk about it sometime?*
Zen Teacher	*Of course! Let us sit and meditate together.*
Christian	*That would be wonderful. When could we do this?*
Zen Teacher	*Right now! Let's begin.*
Christian	*Right now? But where?*
Zen Teacher	*Right here. On this cushion.*
Christian	*Here? For how long?*
Zen Teacher	*All day. Let's begin.*
Christian	*Here? Now? All day? On this cushion?*
Zen Teacher	*Of course, you said you were interested.*
Christian	*Well yes. But I hadn't planned to do it just now. I thought we could talk about it and I could hear about your experience.*
Zen Teacher	*Let's begin. Do it! Do it now!* [22]

A Simple Guide to the Church's Year

Advent
There are four Sundays in the season of Advent, which starts around the beginning of December.

Christmas
There may be two Sundays in the Christmas season.

Epiphany
The season of Epiphany has four Sundays and begins on the feast of the Epiphany (6 January) and ends at the feast of the Presentation of Christ in the Temple or Candlemas (2 February).

Lent, Holy Week and Easter
Following the feast of the Presentation of Christ, there can follow up to five 'Sundays before Lent'. Lent itself begins on Ash Wednesday which is forty days before Palm Sunday and the beginning of Holy Week, which ends on Easter Day.

Easter to Pentecost
There are seven Sundays in the season of Easter which consists of the fifty days leading to Pentecost.

Sundays after Trinity
Pentecost is followed by Trinity Sunday, followed by Sundays after Trinity which can be as many as twenty-three. The last Sunday after Trinity which comes at about the end of October may be kept as Bible Sunday or as a Dedication Festival. Readings for a Dedication Festival are the subject for reflection on page 162.

Sundays before Advent
There are four 'Sundays before Advent', the last of which is the feast of Christ the King. This is followed by Advent Sunday, which marks the beginning of the next year.

Week of Advent 1

Stilling and Centring

Take time to enter into stillness and to be still. Use whatever way works for you to take you into worship and adoration – repeating a phrase from the psalm, or a word or phrase you have chosen, or whatever way best helps you.

Psalm 18:1   *I love you, O Lord my strength,*
O Lord my crag, my fortress, and my deliverer.

Offering

At the end of your silence offer your day that God's kingdom may come in the lives of the people you will meet and the situations on your mind. Offer any action or activity, meetings or relationships, that you may be part of God's redeeming purposes.

Reflecting

As you have time during the week, reflect on Luke 21:25-36.

The Church's year begins with an apocalyptic passage which reflects the belief of the time about the imminent coming of the 'Son of Man' and the end of the world. However we interpret the precise meaning, the stress on the need for alertness and confidence in the triumphant Mystery of God in a world which at times seems to be descending into chaos is strikingly contemporary. The call, whatever the situation, is to a constant alertness and a looking out for the signs of the One who comes to save, especially in the midst of chaos and disorder.

Don't rush at the passage – give time for meanings to emerge that connect with your experience.

Don't worry about distractions. They will come at you constantly. The mind is incredibly active, shooting off in many directions all the time.

When you discover that you have wandered off again into some memory of the past, or fantasy of the future . . . or worry . . . or imaginary conversation . . . or argument . . . or entertaining daydream . . . gently bring your attention back and focus it again on the word you are silently repeating, the name you are gently naming; determinedly keep it there.

Your mind will wander again, but as you stay with your word in disciplined attentiveness, you will find that the agitation gradually subsides. You discover that without quite knowing how, you have, in the mystery of God, become still.

I said to my soul be still, and wait without hope

For hope would be hope for the wrong thing; wait without love

For love would be love of the wrong thing; there is yet faith

But the faith and the love and the hope are all in the waiting.

Wait without thought, for you are not ready for thought:

So the darkness shall be the light and the stillness the dancing.

'East Coker', The Four Quartets, *T. S. Eliot* [23]

Week of Advent 2

Stilling and Centring

Take time to enter into stillness and to be still. Use whatever way works for you to take you into worship and adoration – a phrase from the psalm, or a word or phrase you have chosen, or whatever way best helps you.

Psalm 63:1   *O God, you are my God, eagerly I seek you;*
my soul thirsts for you, my flesh faints for you
as in a barren and dry land where there is no water.

Offering

Following your silence, offer your day that God's kingdom may come into the situations on your mind. Offer those whom you will meet and any activity in the day ahead, that you may remain alive to the life of God within you.

Reflecting

During the week reflect on Luke 3:1-6.

As well as introducing the figure of the Baptist, the Gospel is a call to prepare for the One who is to come. John proclaims that it is through a baptism of 'repentance' – a turning away from the anxieties of our minds to the unseen Christ – that gradually, imperceptibly, the roughness and crookedness which bedevil us may be healed so that we may *see*, that is, be open to the mysterious presence of God.

Let the meanings you discover in the passage connect with meanings and understandings from your experience.

The discipline of daily meditation simplifies, heals and unites. As we learn to listen to the word and nothing but the word in an attitude of focused attention, we find that a clarifying, simplifying and healing process occurs somewhere deep within us. Anxieties, which can become complex labyrinths of the mind in which we may get lost if we try to analyse them, lose their sharpness. The noisy agitation of the spirit is slowly silenced. We become more at one with the person that we sense we really are.

One writer has described the word as being like the single clear note of the oboe played before a concert begins in order to bring all the other discordant instruments of the orchestra into tune.

So we sound the word. Gradually and gently, the faculties of mind and spirit are integrated and we are brought to a place where we may be ready to receive the Mystery of God.

Abba Evagrius said, 'I was tormented by the thoughts and passions of the body so I went to find Abba Macarius. I said to him, "Father, give me a word to live by." Abba Macarius said to me, "Secure the anchor rope to the rock and by the grace of God the ship will ride the devilish waves of this beguiling sea . . ." I said to him, "What is the boat? What is the rope? What is the rock?" Abba Macarius said to me, "The ship is your heart; keep guard over it. The rope is your mind; secure it to our Lord Jesus Christ, who is the rock who has power over all the waves . . . because it is not difficult, is it, to say with each breath, 'Our Lord Jesus, have mercy on me: I bless thee, my Lord Jesus, help me.'"'

Pseudo-Macarius [24]

Week of Advent 3

Stilling and Centring

Take time to enter into stillness and to be still. Use whatever way works for you to take you into worship and adoration – a phrase from the psalm, or a word or phrase you have chosen, or whatever way best helps you.

Psalm 42:1-2 *As the deer longs for the water-brooks,*
so longs my soul for you, O God.

Offering

As you come gently out of your silence offer your day and your concerns – that you may stay in touch with that sense of longing and searching which is at the heart of what it means to seek the kingdom of God. Offer those whom you will be with – that you may see them as God sees them, with love and compassion.

Reflecting

As you have time during the week, reflect on Luke 3:7-18.

The Gospel continues the theme of preparation and questioning about the Coming One, whom John sees in terms of purifying judgement. He uses the image of a farmer with a winnowing fork in hand, clearing his threshing floor, gathering wheat and burning chaff. It is important to remember that everyone is wheat and in everyone there is chaff; judgement is not a question of destruction but of purifying. With the repeated refrain 'What should we do?', the passage draws attention in vivid detail to the ethical dimensions of being a disciple.

Be attentive with your imagination to the images in this passage and open to any meanings that may emerge.

What is Christianity? A moral improvement? Certainly. A greater capacity given to share, to be honest, to be content with what you have? Yes. But all that is not even the beginning. ·

We dare to expect something more profound.

By patiently and persistently turning our attention away from our own daily concerns and distractions towards the silence and mysterious 'otherness' of God, the promise is that gradually a greater clarity of understanding, a greater capacity to 'see' and a greater stillness of heart and mind will begin to occur within us. This is something of what it means to be 'purified'.

Gradually, through this constant turning towards the source of life an entire moral, spiritual and psychological reorientation of what it means to be a human being will take place – even in us . . .

. . . nothing less than a gentle igniting of the heart . . . *with the Holy Spirit and with fire.*

It takes daily courage to expose oneself to God's word and to allow oneself to be judged by it; it takes daily energy to delight in God's love . . . What shall we do, in order to penetrate into this silence before God? . . . Not one of us lives such a hectic life that he cannot spare the time . . . to be still and let the silence gather round him, to stand in the presence of eternity and to let it speak, to enquire from it about our condition, and to gaze deep into himself and far out . . . beyond and above . . . his soul begins to be replenished and revitalised and to receive strength, then he begins to know the eternal quiet which rests in God's love; stress and anxiety, hurry and restlessness, noise and clamour are stilled within him, he has become silent before God who is his help.

Dietrich Bonhoeffer

Week of Advent 4

Stilling and Centring

Take time to enter into stillness and to be still. Use whatever way works for you to take you into worship and adoration – a phrase from the psalm, or a word or phrase you have chosen, or whatever way best helps you.

Psalm 62:1   *My soul waits in silence for God*
for from him comes my salvation.

Offering

Emerging from your silence offer your day that God's kingdom may come into the lives of the people you will meet and the situations on your mind. Offer any relationship, meeting or activity in the day ahead, that the life of God may be 'magnified' in you – and others.

Reflecting

During the week reflect on Luke 1:39-55.

This is an extraordinarily beautiful passage. The picture of these two pregnant women greeting one another and bursting out in shouts of blessing as the new life within them erupts in joy, is an image of the hidden 'inner' nature of the Life of the Spirit within each of us.

Focus your whole attention on the words and their meanings in you. Let them go deeply into your heart.

I once heard the journey of the prayer time described as being like descending from the surface of the sea to the depths of the ocean in a kind of diving chamber. The turbulent waves on the surface represent the agitated surface of the mind as we respond to everyday pressures. As you begin to be still, and patiently attend to your word, which is like the diving chamber taking you slowly down, you begin to leave the immediate world of agitated thought behind. But as you descend everything below the surface is by no means calm. Some distance down are to be found the huge currents of the ocean. These correspond to the powerful psychological forces that run below the surface of our minds and, often unbeknown to us, drive and shape what we do and how we behave. Here can be found our need to succeed, our addiction to work, our fear of emptiness, our craving for recognition, our fear of failure; powerful forces that drive us on and make us the people we wish we were often not. In the silence of our prayer, with our minds starved of distractions, we may become freshly and disconcertingly aware of them. However, our persistent faithfulness and attention to the word we say, to the name we name, and nothing else, will take us deeper and away from these too. Eventually we arrive at the bottom of the ocean, to a place where the currents have finally ceased altogether, where it is utterly silent and dark and still. Here there is no movement at all. Here it is possible to rest with a great sense of gratitude. Here God dwells, and in secret, you dwell in him.

Spiritual life gets nowhere without discipline and endurance, a 'rule of prayer' that helps shape each and every day. If you want to make headway in prayer, you pray when you are not in the mood, pray when there is no time, pray even if you have no sense of the presence of God. Prayer is like love of your children – you take care of them and their basic needs no matter how you happen to be feeling at that moment. You slowly build up islands of prayer at the beginning and end of each day until prayer is one of the main structures of life.

Jim Forest [25]

It seems to me we have to have the nerve to pray, and one of the things which is related to praying in a secular age is the recovery of nerve.

David Jenkins [26]

Christmas 1

Stilling and Centring

Take time to be still. Use a phrase from the psalm, or a word or phrase you have chosen, or follow your own path into stillness and adoration.

Psalm 36:9 *With you is the well of life,*
and in your light shall we see light.

Offering

Following your silence, offer your day and all that you plan to do. Offer any who you may meet whom you sense are particularly searching for the Life of God even though they may not be very aware of it. Offer your relationship with them.

Reflecting

During the week reflect on Luke 2:41-52.

Full of human detail, this story contains hints of Luke's other stories of searching for that which is lost in Chapter 15. At the heart of it is the question of the identity of Jesus who is clearly no ordinary boy, but feels himself to be under an inner compulsion – 'Did you now know that I must be in my Father's house?' The harassed parents, turning away from the crowd and going in search of him who is lost to them, are a picture of us all. At the end Mary again ponders the enigma of her son: Who is he, so poised and centred in 'his Father's house' untroubled by the furore around him?

And her anxiety gives way to wonder.

The prayer time is the daily effort whatever we may feel – and always there is something solitary about it – of turning away from the crowd and going in search of that which is our life but which we somehow can no longer find.

Harassed and agitated, the Word initially acts simply as a focus in the midst of a jumble of chaotic thoughts. But as we stay with it, and refuse to be side-tracked, it leads us on, until occasionally, and for a moment, the awareness may break through that our sense of lostness is an illusion. And like the first rays of the sun dawning upon us, we realise that in the Mystery of the Love of God, we always and eternally belong.

And anxiety gives way to wonder.

Later on I began to have daily pilgrimages to think these things. There was a feeling that I must go somewhere, and be alone. It was a necessity to have a few minutes of this separate life every day; my mind required to live its own life apart from other things. A great oak at a short distance was one resort, and sitting in the grass at its roots, or leaning against the trunk and looking over the quiet meadows towards the bright southern sky, I could live my own life a little while.

Richard Jefferies [27]

There is only one problem on which all my existence, my peace and my happiness depend; to discover myself in discovering God. If I find him, I will find myself; and if I find my true self, I will find him.

Thomas Merton [28]

Christmas 2

Stilling and Centring

Take time to be still. Use a phrase from the psalm, or a word or phrase you have chosen, or follow your own path into stillness and adoration.

Psalm 86:11-12 *Teach me your way, O Lord*
and I will walk in your truth.

Offering

Coming out of your silence, offer your day that you may be alert to the 'way' of God in all that you do. Offer those with whom you will spend time this day, this week.

Reflecting

During the week reflect on John 1:1-11.

This beginning, with the repeated phrase, 'came into being' takes us back to the miracle of life itself – the amazing fact that anything exists at all and not nothing! But the passage does more than celebrate the miracle of biological life, it opens up the mystery of what it means to be, to have a 'soul' – a spiritual and moral centre that responds to God and can give itself away in love. This love is the key to the meaning of the universe. The good news is that this Mystery of Being, of self-transcending love which began everything has lived amongst us, in the man Jesus. John saw his glory and so can anyone see and share in this glory – who believes.

The task of prayer is particularly important if you feel that the natural foundations of your life are shaky, have been shot away or pulled to bits by neglect, abuse, emotional violence, or simple and persistent disrespect from your early years; a disrespect that you have perhaps tragically and disastrously internalised.

After you have talked or wept this out, you will come to understand yourself to some degree and the reason why your behaviour can sometimes be so difficult. After you have worked it through a bit you need to find a different kind of rootedness to that which you previously experienced.

And that is what praying can give you – a rootedness and belonging in the unconditional acceptance and love of God.

That is what your prayer can lead you to – day by day.

God gives birth to his only begotten Son in you . . . If you wait for this birth in you, then you find all goodness and all consolation, all bliss, all being and all truth . . . For it brings you pure being and steadfastness.

Meister Eckhart [29]

(Anthony) called his two companions . . . and said to them 'Always breathe Christ.'

Athanasius of Alexandria [30]

To be rooted is perhaps the most important and least recognised need of the human soul.

Simone Weil [31]

Epiphany 1

Stilling and Centring

Take time to be still. Use a phrase from the psalm, or a word or phrase you have chosen, or follow your own path into stillness and adoration.

Psalm 84:5   *Blessed is the one whose strength is in you,*
in whose heart are the highways to Zion.

Offering

Following your silence offer your day. Grounded in your word or phrase from the psalm, pray that you may know your identity as a beloved child of God throughout this day or week. Give thanks for the sense of the strength of the Life of God.

Reflecting

During the week reflect on Luke 3:15-17, 21-22.

What is striking is the contrast between the fearsome imagery of the preaching of John with its overtones of judgement – 'winnowing fork' and 'unquenchable fire' and the dawning reign of grace in Jesus, identifying himself with the people as he goes down to be baptised and, emerging with heaven opening, to be affirmed as 'the Beloved Son'.

Take time to allow the meanings you find in the passage to connect with meanings in your life.

We are creatures of habit. Our lives are structured round things that we have to do: work, administration, keeping the house clean, doing the shopping; and the things we enjoy doing: eating, cooking, watching TV, going on holiday, being with friends.

Prayer is neither of these. That is why it is so difficult to get it established in our lives.

We neither have to do it, nor usually do we want to do it. In fact we shall very likely keep on trying to avoid it, finding any excuse not to do it.

And yet we know that unless we do it, our lives will shrivel. Our capacity to give to others will diminish, and we shall go on tripping up over the same faults and blunders that have dogged us for years. Or we shall quietly grow dull.

In a word we shall not be the people we are meant to be.

So we have to choose to pray each day. And each day it is hard.

God created the human being, bringing its body forth from the pre-existing matter which he animated with his own Spirit . . . Thus in some way a new universe was born, small and great at one and the same time. God set this 'hybrid' worshipper on earth to contemplate the visible world and to be initiated into the invisible . . . He created a being at once earthly and heavenly, insecure and immortal, visible and invisible, half-way between greatness and nothingness, flesh and spirit at the same time . . . an animal en route to another native land . . .

Gregory Nazianzen [32]

Epiphany 2

Stilling and Centring

Take time to be still. Use a phrase from the psalm, or a word or phrase you have chosen, or follow your own path into stillness and adoration.

Psalm 36:7   *How priceless is your love, O God;*
your people take refuge under the shadow of your wings.

Offering

In the strength of the silence offer your concerns and your day, that you may be an instrument of God's peace, open and alert to the transforming power and presence of the Gospel, in you and in others.

Reflecting

During the week reflect on John 2:1–11.

With the words 'on the third day there was a wedding . . .', this first of Jesus' seven great signs in the Gospel of John points forward to something else that will happen 'on the third day', when everything is to be transformed.

The story is richly symbolic. The wine runs out suggesting an end to the dispensation of the Jews, now exhausted. 'Do whatever he tells you' – the Jewish mother acknowledges the authority of her Son. The use of the six stone jars which are to be full of wine points towards the end of ritual washing away of sins. But water suggests more: it is the raw material of all creation (the Spirit hovered over the face of the waters in Genesis). We are told 'they filled them to the brim', suggesting that in this Son everything, all creation, is to be transformed. The steward congratulates the bridegroom on the new wine, but we know that another hidden bridegroom has created this wine. The question lingers: who will be the bride?

Allow your imagination to work on the detail of this story and the meanings you find.

Our lives are often pallid, insubstantial, and sometimes constantly apologetic. Too easily we get caught up in anxious repetitions of guilt and apology, arising not so much out of what we do, as from what we think we are, such can be the degree of our self-doubt.

To pray means a determined turning away from that kind of empty and depressive self-understanding which at times invades and overwhelms like a great grey cloud. Instead it is a persistent focusing of consciousness away from our needy emptiness, to the One in whom we need to learn simply to rest – and to be.

The patient and determined practice of this turning, this resting, this being, leads to the discovery of a new kind of self . . . a rested, strengthened and freed heart, strangely given . . .

. . . no longer water – but wine.

. . . contemplation is entirely a matter of attention – that is, doing the practice in as unselfconscious a manner as possible, because the quality of the attention counts for so much. If one is simply satisfied with the natural tranquillity yielded up by acquired contemplation, then one is satisfied with a half-baked practice that may go quickly rancid. The essence of a mature practice is to lose the self in the practice.

Gregory Mayers [33]

Attention . . . is the root of all our inner spiritual life.

Theophan the Recluse [34]

Epiphany 3

Stilling and Centring

Take time to be still. Use a phrase from the psalm, or a word or phrase you have chosen, or follow your own path into stillness and adoration.

Psalm 57:8   *My heart is fixed, O God, my heart is fixed;*
I will sing and make melody.

Offering

Out of the silence of your worship gently focus your mind on the people and concerns you face in the coming day or week, and offer them to God, that the freedom and life of the kingdom may come into their lives.

Reflecting

During the week reflect on Luke 4:14-21.

This passage which Luke places right at the beginning of Jesus' ministry has been called the 'Nazareth Manifesto' as it spells out his programme and purpose. It is notable that he ends his reading from Isaiah at the word 'favour' so leaving out the last line which continues, 'and the day of vengeance of our God'.

In this man, the reign of grace has fully dawned; the note of judgement heard in the preaching of the Baptist is gone.

Praying is the disciplined work of learning to 'fix' what has been called 'the eye of the heart' beyond oneself – onto the Mystery and Presence of Christ.

It is extraordinary how, if you persist in a steadfast and determined focusing of your mind, gently repeating your word of adoration, a slow process of releasing begins to occur within you. Continue to gently repeat your word of adoration in time with your breath and in tune with your heart, until you and your word may even seem to become one.

It is hard work at first, this 'work of God'. But if we persist in it, those things that have restricted and oppressed us – fears, anxieties, worries, neuroses – gradually lose the power of their grip. They lighten and may even dissolve entirely. A new kind of freedom and peace of heart is born within.

It is a great gift; and you find you emerge from your practice quietly more alive – and able to act.

The 'ever-increasing predominance of Action over Activity' – the deep and vital movement of the whole self, too utterly absorbed for self-consciousness, set over against its fussy surface-energies – here is the true ideal of orison (prayer). This must inform all the soul's aspiration towards union with the absolute Life and Love which waits at the door.

Evelyn Underhill with a quotation from Baron von Hugel [35]

Epiphany 4

Stilling and Centring

Take time to be still. Use a phrase from the psalm, or a word or phrase you have chosen, or follow your own path into stillness and adoration.

Psalm 48:8   *We have waited in silence*
              on your loving kindness, O God.

Offering

As you turn towards your day offer yourself that you may learn to wait for God this day, for his kingdom to come in the lives of those around you and in your own life with them. Offer any who are especially on your mind.

Reflecting

During the week reflect on Luke 2:22-40.

The Presentation of Christ in the Temple (Candlemas) which the Church of England keeps on the fourth Sunday of Epiphany, takes us back into Jesus' infancy and to two devout old people who had been waiting all their lives for 'the consolation of Israel'. At the heart of the Gospel is the Nunc Dimittis, a great cry of fulfilment – at last the consolation has come. The coming means both the consolation of Israel and, for this faithful old man, the end of long years of patient believing. His faith is finally vindicated. The tone is one of triumphant but humble gratitude. Cradling the child in his arms he exclaims, 'My eyes have seen . . . !'

Prayer can mean long periods of waiting and believing, often in darkness; but in the end, God will always come.

We live in a world which has largely forgotten how to wait.

Perhaps that is one reason why we find prayer so difficult for it means continuing to seek the presence of God long after the first glow of enthusiasm has died away; and you may have begun to wonder whether this praying thing is doing any good at all, to you or anybody else. There will be days when nothing seems to 'happen'. Those are the times when you need to trust a hidden process of growth that is going on in and through your discipline but below the surface of your consciousness – like the roots of a plant silently forming.

And then at some brief moment, and perhaps only for a moment, something dawns in you – a vivid moment of awareness, perceptiveness, understanding, wonder, joy . . .

. . . *my eyes have seen* . . . the world . . . everything around you . . . other people – lit up, beautiful and glorious.

. . . we see in our own beauty the image of the godhead . . . You have in you the ability to see God.

Gregory of Nyssa [36]

The whole purpose of this life is to restore to health the eye of the heart whereby God may be seen.

Augustine of Hippo [37]

Sunday between 3 and 9 February
(if earlier than the Second Sunday before Lent)

Stilling and Centring

Take time to be still. Use a phrase from the psalm, or a word or phrase you have chosen, or follow your own path into stillness and adoration.

Psalm 138:1   *I will give thanks to you, O Lord,*
with my whole heart.

Offering

In the strength of the silence offer your day and your concerns. As you become aware of those who you are to meet or work with this day, be thankful for them.

Reflecting

During the week reflect on Luke 5:1-11.

At the heart of this passage is the experience of being overwhelmed, one's own fruitless efforts being completely swamped by something extraordinary. In a rare moment, you are jerked right out of yourself and the limitations of your small, well-tried world. The nets start breaking . . . the boat begins to sink.

When this God of surprises comes visiting there can be all kinds of responses: astonishment and disbelief, shame at one's perennial pessimism and hopelessness; and fear in the face of the reality of this kingdom. We need to hear again and again 'Do not be afraid'; and 'Put out into the deep', so that we may discover what this God will do with our so limited under-standing of living, loving and praying.

Prayer is normally the daily, weekly task of 'abiding' – the business of just sticking at it, with occasional 'consolation'.

And then there may be a visitation. Quite suddenly emptiness becomes fullness; searching gives way to finding.

Such rare and precious moments are just given; though paradoxically they are more likely to be given as we faithfully go on labouring 'to enter into rest' as the author of the letter to the Hebrews puts it.

The working all night with nothing caught, and finding the nets bulging the next morning may, after all, be more connected than we thought.

Fear not the coming of your God; fear not his friendship. He will not straiten you when he comes; rather he will enlarge you.

Augustine of Hippo [38]

What do I care about heaven when I myself have become heaven.

John Chrysostom [39]

Sunday between 10 and 16 February
(if earlier than the Second Sunday before Lent)

Stilling and Centring

Take time to be still. Use a phrase from the psalm, or a phrase you have chosen, or follow your own path into stillness.

Psalm 1:1, 2, 3   *Happy are those . . . whose delight is in the law of the Lord, and on his law they meditate day and night; they are like trees planted by streams of water . . .*

Offering

Become aware of what you are to face in the coming day or week and simply offer it in the confidence of the kingdom of God. Offer any you know who are poor, hungry, or who are in grief.

Reflecting

During the week reflect on Luke 6:17-26.

'If you will present yourself with your need only . . .' the door to the kingdom of God opens within us to the extent that we are able to acknowledge the degree of our emptiness and longing, and the muddle of our lives that drives us to prayer. We are incomplete, alienated people, cut off from the Ground of our life, and we need help.

As you read these phrases from the Lukan beatitudes, repeat them slowly so that they go deep into your mind. Meditate on them 'day and night' as the psalmist suggests. Let them teach you the joyful, but challenging meaning of the kingdom – in your life.

The repeated cries: 'Lord Jesus Christ' . . . 'Abba, Father' . . . 'Christ have mercy' may be words of adoration but they are also cries for help – the shouts of human beings who know that left to themselves they are going to drown.

It is only as we acknowledge our need for grace, and realise that ultimately 'we have no resources of ourselves to help ourselves', that the gift of the kingdom may come.

Prayer is learning to step out of the proud illusion of our self-sufficiency and to say from the depths of us: 'Kyrie Eleison . . . Lord have mercy upon me.'

The Kingdom

It's a long way off but inside it
There are quite different things going on:
Festivals at which the poor man
Is King and the consumptive is
Healed: mirrors in which the blind look
At themselves and love looks at them
Back: and industry is for mending
The bent bones and the minds fractured
By life. It's a long way off, but to get
There takes no time and admission
Is free, if you will purge yourself
Of desire, and present yourself with
Your need only and the simple offering
Of your faith, green as a leaf.

R. S. Thomas [40]

81

Sunday between 17 and 23 February

(if earlier than the Second Sunday before Lent)

Stilling and Centring

Take time to be still. Use a phrase from the psalm, or a word or phrase you have chosen, or follow your own path into stillness and adoration.

Psalm 37:7   *Be still before the Lord
and wait patiently for him.*

Offering

Gently offer what lies ahead that something of the stillness and sense of being-in-God that you have discovered in your silence may stay with you in your day, your week.

Reflecting

During the week reflect on Luke 6:27-38.

The purpose of the Gospel is to set us free from ourselves, our chronic self-attachment which breeds suspicions and fear and may create enemies, and bring us to a state of mind where the well-being of our neighbour matters as much as our own.

Such a turning inside out of the 'natural' priorities of the human mind is possible. It opens the door to the extraordinarily healing discovery that all people – friend or stranger, compatriot or foreigner, of my creed or another creed – all are my brothers and sisters in whom I can find Christ.

As you stay with this passage, let it illuminate your experience, judging and healing.

Every prayer time is one more lesson in the hard school of self-forgetfulness.

As we deliberately forget our needs and anxieties, and instead focus into the void, a kind of dying happens in us as the ego is starved of all attention.

At this point we may feel we have entered a bleak landscape of the spirit, where there is nothing for the mind to attach itself to. Sitting and simply persisting we find that there are no comforts and no consolation in this praying. We are accompanied by nothing but the intuition that somehow, despite all the evidence of our feelings, we are on the right path and our time is not entirely being wasted.

Persisting in this narrow way, we may begin to discover the first intimations of another self being given back to us — somehow stronger, more solid, and less needy than that which we have so painfully left behind.

The purpose of contemplation is neither to improve our morals or ethics nor to perfect our personality to win friends and influence people, nor any kind of self-improvement or self-aggrandising goal. The 'purpose' of contemplation is to lose our self . . .

Gregory Mayers [41]

Second Sunday before Lent

Stilling and Centring

Take time to be still. Use a phrase from the psalm, or a word or phrase you have chosen, or follow your own path into stillness and adoration.

Psalm 19:14 *Let the words of my mouth and meditations of my heart*
be acceptable in your sight,
O Lord, my strength and my redeemer.

Offering

Let your offering grow out of your silence. Offer those who you know particularly need the strength of God. Offer all who struggle to find strength in difficult pain-filled situations.

Reflecting

During the week reflect on Luke 8:22-25.

The narrative is a vivid exploration of faith and doubt. It speaks of the experience of the absence of God, and the fear, panic and bewilderment that we so easily feel when our lives are being overwhelmed by events that we cannot control.

As you reflect on this passage be aware of those things that produce fear and panic in you, and hear the question of Jesus of Nazareth addressed to you.

Let your imagination work on the image of Christ at the centre of a huge calm and stillness. Take the image into your world.

As we come to prayer we may feel that we are little more than a bundle of chaotic and anxious noise. Like passengers on an overloaded train, anxieties, obligations, fears and hopes jostle one another within us, vying and competing for attention.

Sitting still, attending to the word and nothing else, gradually stills this cacophony.

As we persist, focusing on a word, we may have the strange experience of coming upon a kind of foundation that we had no idea was there – some kind of inner rock . . . and we know deeply, beyond words, something of who we really are.

Being itself exists in us, whose name is Christ, God.

We become God in so far as we lose ourselves. If God is truly to speak to you, then all the energies of your soul must be silent. It is not a question of learning to do but of learning not to do.

Johannes Tauler [42]

The heart that is freed from imaginings ends up by producing in itself holy and mysterious thoughts, as on a calm sea you see fish leaping and dolphins gambolling.

Hesychius of Batos [43]

Sunday next before Lent

Stilling and Centring

Take time to be still. Use a phrase from the psalm, or a word or phrase you
have chosen, or follow your own path into stillness and adoration.

Psalm 43:3 *Send out your light and your truth that they may lead me
and bring me to your holy hill and to your dwelling.*

Offering

Offer your day and your concerns that you may be led into deeper understandings and greater love for those you meet, that you and they may be
'brought' to the place where God dwells.

Reflecting

During the week reflect on Luke 9:28-36.

This passage is about persistence in praying and what can happen when we
determinedly 'stay awake'.

It is also about the need to guard the 'holy fire' within. Luke tells us, 'The
disciples kept silent and in those days told no one of the things they had
seen . . .' Sometimes this mysterious and hidden Gospel needs to remain
hidden.

The tragedy of our days is that for most of the time we miss it – the glory hidden everywhere.

We are 'weighed down' with 'sleep' – the condition of the mindless and unaware.

We are terrified of the cloud – the realm of not knowing.

We shatter the silence with empty words.

But despite ourselves we are what St Basil called 'an animal en route to another land', to 'theosis' which means 'deification' . . . God-like.

The kingdom of God, they say, is within you; seek it then in the most secret habitations of the soul. The mystic must learn so to concentrate all his faculties, his very self, upon the invisible and intangible, that all visible things are forgot: to bring it so sharply into focus that everything else is blurred. He must call in his scattered faculties by a deliberate exercise of the will, empty the mind of its swarm of images, its riot of thoughts. In mystical language he 'must sink into his nothingness'; into that blank abiding place where busy, clever Reason cannot come.

Evelyn Underhill [44]

Lent 1

Stilling and Centring

Take time to be still. Use a phrase from the psalm, or a word or phrase you have chosen, or follow your own path into stillness and adoration.

Psalm 91:2   *You are my refuge and my strength,*
my God in whom I put my trust.

Offering

In this first week of Lent, simply offer the time ahead right up to Holy Week that you may find a deeper 'refuge' – and strength for others. Offer your day.

Reflecting

During the week reflect on Luke 4:1-13.

After affirmation and glory the testing begins.

The three-fold response of Jesus points to all that is needed for the full blossoming of a spiritual life: 'One does not live by bread alone . . .'; 'worship the Lord your God and serve only him . . .'; and the third which points to the path of not knowing but just believing: 'Do not put the Lord your God to the test.'

Pray these texts of the Gospel into your heart. What is their meaning in your life?

Much of our prayer is a subtle kind of bargaining game: We will pray, a little and from time to time, if we are rewarded, answered, protected, and guided.

To go to your room, and focus the mind in the silent discipline of your practice, is to seek God for himself alone.

Then prayer, instead of being a thinly disguised process of spiritual calculation, becomes the daily offering of a gift . . .

. . . our muddled selves just longing.

It is almost impossible to do this without a ritual. Ritual makes this difficult task easier. Ritual allows us to learn how to learn. What do we learn? Non-attachment to the self-trance, the ego identity. We learn one skill, posture, breathing, breath counting, a skill that can be taught, so that we can learn another skill that can only be caught: attention, non-attachment. Contrary to the popular notion, spontaneity is the fruit of discipline, not a substitute for it.

Gregory Mayers [45]

Lent 2

Stilling and Centring

Take time to be still. Use a phrase from the psalm, or a word or phrase you have chosen, or follow your own path into stillness and adoration.

Psalm 27:1 *The Lord is my light and my salvation,*
whom then shall I fear?
The Lord is the strength of my life,
of whom then shall I be afraid?

Offering

Offer your day and your concerns, that you may be freer from that of which you are so habitually afraid. Offer all who are beset by fear and anxiety.

Reflecting

During the week reflect on Luke 13:31-56.

This passage is full of the anguish and longing of Christ in the face of the stubborn obduracy of the world, and is shot through with double meaning.

Everything in the Gospels is written in the light of Easter. Raised 'on the third day' neither Herod nor the Pharisees have any power over this One who 'finished his work' in his rising.

Every human being potentially shares in that triumph, but we are 'not willing'.

To think that *we* pray is a delusion.

Fencing off time and emptying the mind simply creates space for the Spirit to pray in us. So as we are still we find that we are gently gathered up in the interchange of love at the heart of this trinitarian God . . .

. . . and we become part of the adoring.

Prayer is among the most persistent and universal of human activities . . . Yet we live in a secular age that tends to regard prayer as having a decorative social function – possible comforting for some but non-essential. Secularism . . . is the negation of the human being as homo adorans, the being for whom worship is the most essential action, that which makes us truly human. It is our God-given nature to pray, but in a secular society, those who pray may have to endure being thought of as odd.

From Praying with Icons, *Jim Forest* [46]

Lent 3

Stilling and Centring

Take time to be still. Use a phrase from the psalm, or a word or phrase you have chosen, or follow your own path into stillness and adoration.

Psalm 63:7 *You have been my helper*
and under the shadow of your wings will I rejoice.

Offering

There is a kind of secret delight at the heart of this praying business. Offer your day with the prayer that you may not lose that delight in, and through, all that you have to face.

Reflecting

During the week reflect on Luke 13:1-9.

The first part of this reading appears stark and frightening with its vivid pictures of violent death and the refrain: 'Unless you repent you will all perish . . .'

The parable of the fig tree illuminates the meaning: to repent is to face the challenge of simply being the people that we already are – but have forgotten. The root fact of our existence is that we 'live and move and have our being' in God. Our sin is that we forget it and try to live apart from him. To repent is to remember – to re-member ourselves, to be re-joined to the Ground of life and live from that inner Ground, bearing fruit.

To repeat the holy name of God in focused adoration is one deceptively simple way to be re-membered.

As we sit in the silence of our room starved of all distractions, a slow and hidden process of re-connecting takes place in the forgotten depths of who we are.

Though our minds scarcely know it, we are in fact 'repenting', and through our discipline finding the slow miracle of life returning.

'Little by little . . . prayer has to make a void that waits on God, an attentive, recollected, loving void. A void where the internal straining has nothing external corresponding to it,' says Simone Weil. Poverty. 'Nada' of the Spanish mystics.

Olivier Clément [47]

Therefore I will leave on one side everything I can think, and choose for my love that thing which I cannot think.

The Cloud of Unknowing [48]

Lent 4

Stilling and Centring

Take time to be still. Use a phrase from the psalm, or a word or phrase you have chosen, or follow your own path into stillness and adoration.

Psalm 32:8   *You are a place to hide me in,*
you will preserve me from trouble,
you will surround me with deliverance on every side.

Offering

As you turn outwards to the day ahead, offer all whom you will meet and all that you will do in the strength of your sense of belonging to God.

Reflecting

During the week reflect on Luke 15:1-3, 11b-32.

It may be 'Mothering Sunday' in the Church of England, but don't miss time to reflect deeply on this story which, more than any other, takes us to the heart of the Gospel.

In the centre of the picture is the waiting father – who releases life as a gift, is full of compassion, is not interested in past sins, and throws a giant party at the return of his beloved son. We are that prodigal. We are also the son who works 'like a slave', who cannot believe that, in the household of God, life is always a gift to be received, and can never be earned.

Take time with this story; what are its meanings in your life?

To determinedly embrace the name of Christ, or to let the phrase of a psalm go deeper and deeper in you, is to hear, at first from far away, the faint sound of a huge party – the notes of music and the rhythm of dancing. It is to pick up, at first just faintly on the wind, the distant noise of celebration and delight.

The one who is being cheered home is you.

Gradually through the persistence of prayer we join in the celebration of our own loveliness, created as we are in his image; an image forgotten and denied as we went on behaving 'like a slave'.

In the house of God it is always a holiday.

Olivier Clement [49]

As freedom uncoils within the human person we are challenged to see life as a process of divinisation.

Laurence Freeman [50]

Lent 5 (Passion Sunday)

Stilling and Centring

Take time to be still. Use a phrase from the psalm, or a word or phrase you
have chosen, or follow your own path into stillness and adoration.

Psalm 27:11   *You speak in my heart and say 'seek my face'.*
Your face, Lord, will I seek.

Offering

Offer your day and your concerns that in every situation you may continue
to 'seek the face' of God.

Reflecting

During the week reflect on John 12:1-8.

At the heart of this story on 'Passion Sunday' is an act of adoration, intimacy and total trust in the face of what seems an utterly hopeless future.
Religion that is alive and fruitful is not about keeping commandments or
even doing good to the poor. It is about losing your heart.

There is always the danger of your practice growing stale and weary, particularly if you are trying too hard. It is easy to forget that you are engaged in an affair of the heart.

Sometimes its repetitive nature does mean that without realising it, distractions have overcome you; the heart's focus has become lost and words have become wooden. Your practice which had seemed so life-giving has withered to a meaningless noise of the mind with only commitment keeping you to it.

It may be that you need to rest.

And then gently focus again, allowing your heart's imagination to be rekindled, until you find that a practice which had become so lifeless is transformed once again into an Epiphany as you meet the miracle of yourself returning: lost and found.

Adoration draws us away from sentiment into that which we adore.

Terry Tastard [51]

. . . the soul that seeks God . . . is no longer anything but gazing.

Pseudo-Macarius [52]

97

Palm Sunday

Stilling and Centring

Take time to be still. Use a phrase from the psalm, or a word or phrase you have chosen, or follow your own path into stillness and adoration.

Psalm 31:16   *Make your face to shine upon your servant*
and in your loving-kindness save me.

Offering

Offer the week ahead, all that you do and are, and all whom you will meet. Offer all those who are persecuted for the cause of right.

Reflecting

During the week reflect on Luke 19:28-40.

The climactic moment. Three long years of living closely with this extraordinary man had welded them heart and soul to him. They had hung on his teaching, wondered at his healings, been ignited by his passion, drunk from his wisdom, adored his presence. Now he was to enter the Holy City to claim his kingdom – not in secret as so often before, but openly, at the time of Passover. They were ecstatic. The devotion in them burst like a dam, but they had no idea of the failure, tragedy and disaster that was about to engulf them as they danced and bellowed their praises.

Faith needs its ecstatic beginnings but is not truly born until it has faced the dark night of loss.

Exuberant joy in religion does not tend to come easily to the contemplative mind.

In his book *Zen Spirit – Christian Spirit*, Robert Kennedy reminds us of its importance. He describes how he was touring the Holy Land with a group of pilgrims. As they were approaching Jerusalem, suddenly their Israeli guide stood up in the bus and shouted: 'Sing, you must sing. No one goes to Jerusalem except in song.' And so, sing we did. We sang all the hymns we could remember until we passed through the gates of the city. In singing, we fulfilled the words of the Talmud that one should not stand up to pray while in a state of sorrow, idleness, laughter, chatter, frivolity, or idle talk, but only in a state of joy.'[53]

So sing we must, even when we hear the sound of the bough cracking, the tree falling.

We are citizens of two worlds . . . the temporal is the world of work and worry, the world that is too much with us. But we have other experiences, brief ecstasies . . . still moments when we enter a kingdom. Then we cease to do. We simply are. Being silences and subdues doing and the temporal melts into the eternal.

Hugh Lavery [54]

Easter Day

Stilling and Centring

Take time to be still. Use a phrase from the psalm, or a word or phrase you have chosen, or follow your own path into stillness and adoration.

Psalm 118:17   *I shall not die but live*
                  and declare the works of the Lord.

Offering

Offer yourself in this Easter week and all whom you will meet that you may be a bearer of Christ to others.

Reflecting

During the week reflect on John 20:1-18.

We will not see unless we search, not hiding from sorrow. Peter and the beloved disciple run, and Mary who stands alone weeping bends down and 'looks in'. 'For whom are you looking?' – the words of Jesus, almost his last in this Gospel, echo his first to Andrew – 'What are you looking for?'

At the beginning and at the end, faith will always be a search for that which is lost. And the search may well take us into and through the darkness of our sorrows.

Easter is about seeking – and finding, and being found, as we are eternally known by name: 'Mary'. And as we are known, so we come to know – a knowledge too deep for words – that God is, and we are, and in him always will be. The Father of Jesus who raised him, is our Father too. And will raise us also. Alleluia.

Out of the silence of the heart's dark cave,
hollowed by sorrow for the world's defeat,
Christ comes victorious, death dead behind him.

And the first word uttered of this new creation
is yours and mine and everyone's name.

And so we know, beyond words,
that 'all shall be well, and all shall be well,
and all manner of things shall be well.'

The sanctified person is someone no longer separated. And he is only sanctified to the extent that he understands in practice that he is no longer separated from anyone or anything. He bears humanity in himself, all human beings in their passion and resurrection. He is identified, in Christ, with the 'whole Adam' . . . He is infinitely vulnerable to the horror of the world, to the tragedies of history being constantly renewed. But he is crushed with Christ and rises again with him, with everyone. He knows that resurrection has the last word. Deeper than horror is the Joy.

Olivier Clément [55]

Easter 2

Stilling and Centring

Take time to be still. Use a phrase from the psalm, or a word or phrase you have chosen, or follow your own path into stillness and adoration.

Psalm 118:14   *The Lord is my strength and my song and has become my salvation.*

Offering

Offer yourself for the coming day that you may remain alive in Christ — open, not defensive, and sensitive and vulnerable to others.

Reflecting

During the week reflect on John 20:19-31.

The terror and fear leading to doors slammed, locked and bolted, is dispelled by the greeting 'Peace be with you', spoken again and again into the heart of panic.

But the emphasis is on the wounds teaching us that only when we are vulnerable, and share the burden of our hurt and pain does Christ live amongst us.

Faith in the resurrection of Jesus Christ is never a triumphant crusade, but the opening up in love and acceptance of hearts that are hurt and afraid, so bringing peace, and removing sins.

Occasionally in the carvings and frescoes of Mediterranean churches there are depictions of the risen Christ descending into hell to visit those imprisoned there.

To a greater or lesser degree all of us share that fate, locked in the prisons of our prejudices, minds set and doors to the new slammed tight. What we see through our bars is the distortion of our projections, the creation of our fears.

Christ will go on visiting the prisoners until the end of time, sharing the wounds that fear causes, turning the key, breathing again, 'Peace be with you . . .', and sending us out into the new and unknown.

(Christ speaks)

I have opened the gates that were bolted,

I have shattered the bars of iron and the iron has become red-hot;

It has melted at my presence; and nothing more has been shut.

Because I am the gate for all beings,

I went to free the prisoners; they belong to me

And I abandon no one . . .

I have sown my fruits in the hearts (of mortals)

And I have changed them into myself . . .

They are my members, and I am their head.

Glory to thee, Lord Christ, our Head! Alleluia!

Odes of Solomon [56]

Easter 3

Stilling and Centring

Take time to be still. Use a phrase from the psalm, or a word or phrase you have chosen, or follow your own path into stillness and adoration.

Psalm 30:13   *My heart sings to you without ceasing*
O Lord my God, I will give you thanks for ever.

Offering

As you face the day or week ahead seek to see each person you meet, and the situations you face, as Christ would. Offer yourself that you may remain alive in his compassion and understanding and truth.

Reflecting

During the week reflect on John 21:1-19.

Allow your imagination to work on the rich detail of this story: the lostness, aimlessness and emptiness in the disciples who 'catch nothing'. Christ there in the silence of the early morning, 'just after daybreak', but unknown and unrecognised. Then the moment of breakthrough – hearing, seeing, recognition. And the return to the Source, the offering of work and the invitation to feed. Understanding and awe combine in receiving the gift of his life. And then the sending out with the three-fold affirmation of love which Simon Peter himself must pronounce again and again, thus nailing forever any lingering guilt at the sound of a cockcrow. And finally the charge for the task ahead – as you have been fed, so feed others.

Take time to see this story in your imagination, to get into the fabric of it. Take it into your heart and life.

Again and again our praying begins from a place far away, turbulent, dark, and empty: the night.

Like the slow and repetitive rhythm of the casting of the empty net on the sea's silent surface, we go again and again in search of a Life from which we are estranged.

And often there is nothing.

But sometimes, there is beyond the night's dark emptiness, the faint echo of a call and a first glimmer of recognition. And we know we have embarked again on the way of return – a return where in the arriving and coming home and resting and feeding, awe and familiarity mingle . . .

. . . and love undergirds everything.

Deep within Shinto temples in Japan you find only a mirror. It is a symbol and a riddle. The risk there is of turning in upon the Self. But the Christian knows that the Self is the image of Christ. And Christ is the faithful mirror who reflects the truth not only of creatures and objects, but also of the Self that is no longer an undifferentiated abyss but the interior expression of a face.

Olivier Clément [57]

Easter 4

Stilling and Centring

Take time to be still. Use a phrase from the psalm, or a word or phrase you have chosen, or follow your own path into stillness and adoration.

Psalm 23:1   *The Lord is my Shepherd*
I shall not be in want.

Offering

Offer your day that you may be alert to the intimations of the Spirit of Christ within you and amongst others. Offer yourself that you may remain trusting that you will indeed not be wanting, and that what you need will be given.

Reflecting

During the week reflect on John 10:22-30.

In the narrative of John things are reaching fever pitch. The next verse tells us 'they took up stones again to stone him'. The final showdown is not far away. What maddens them is that this man says he is 'at one' with God just as earlier he has said that his followers are 'at one' with him.

This intimate oneness with the Divine is the new and offensive promise, and reality of Jesus Christ. Do we realise it?

'You do not believe because you do not belong . . .'
To pray is to face the question of belief the other way round.
It is to follow the searchings of the soul
more than the questions of the mind;
and letting go of
the cramped strictures of a creed,
to let the separated heart
be knit back again into the deep fabric of Divinity,
which wraps the world around
out of which it has been torn;
and to know, 'beyond knowledge',
a faith whose language is a wide embrace
which needs no argument.

In the splayed windows (of the temple in Ezekiel's vision) the part by which the light enters is only a narrow opening, but the interior part that receives the light is wide. In the same way the souls of those who contemplate see only a feeble gleam of true light and yet everything in them seems to expand widely . . . What they see of eternity in their contemplation is almost nothing, yet it is enough to broaden their inward vision . . . Although they are receiving the light of truth as if through a loophole only, everything in them seems to be broadened.

Olivier Clément [58]

Easter 5

Stilling and Centring

Take time to be still. Use a phrase from the psalm, or a word or phrase you have chosen, or follow your own path into stillness and adoration.

Psalm 23:6   *Surely your goodness and mercy shall follow me*
all the days of my life,
and I will dwell in the house of the Lord for ever.

Offering

Offer your day that you may remain and dwell in the love of Christ, and so be present, attentive, alive, and loving to others – especially those you find difficult. Offer them to God for this day.

Reflecting

During the week reflect on John 13:31-35.

Strangely for a reading in the Easter season, this passage takes us back into Holy Week. Jesus has washed the disciples' feet and foretold his betrayal. Judas leaves, and the moment – 'the hour' – has come. Now the focus of their lives will disappear; now, like us, they will move into the challenge of living without him but loved by him; commanded to love, and by his living spirit, enabled to love.

Though this way of prayer requires a degree of solitude – a regular disappearing act – even away from the presence of those you are close to, it is not in order to cultivate a kind of narcissistic individualism – a private cult of the self.

In fact it is the only path to real community and genuine sharing, as in the solitude of our private space we are gradually set free from our egoism which is what so constantly messes up genuine relationships.

In solitude and silence, with no audience to feed off, the ego withers; and slowly and surely the person who we truly are begins to emerge, loved into being by God . . . and free for others.

Loneliness can be dangerous: it also provides a wonderful opportunity, for it is a necessary element of the inner journey. It is as though in loneliness our path is blocked by a strong steel door. We may hit at it, kick against it in rage and frustration, damaging and destroying ourselves, or we may accept that we are blocked and knock gently on the door. The door opens and we enter the inner chamber of our being. There loneliness is transformed into aloneness, which has a very different feel, a feeling of at-one-ness, which banishes the pain of loneliness and makes of solitude a nurture; then, no parting from another ever feels final, for we have entered the inner sanctuary where we, and all creation, are held in being and at one.

Gerard W. Hughes [59]

Easter 6

Stilling and Centring

Take time to be still. Use a phrase from the psalm, or a word or phrase you have chosen, or follow your own path into stillness and adoration.

Psalm 32:9   *I will instruct you and teach you*
in the way that you should go,
I will guide you with my eye.

Offering

Offer your day that you may be alert to the possibility of unknown ways and new things. As you reflect on those you will be with, offer them and their needs.

Reflecting

Reflect on John 14:23-29.

Read back a few verses – particularly to verse 15: 'I will ask the Father and he will give you another Advocate to be with you for ever . . . he will be in you.' This passage suggests an extraordinary intimacy at the heart of the contemplative life. The breathtaking promise is that somehow the very life of the Trinity will come and 'make our home' within those who love God.

If we can begin even to glimpse this then the Peace of verse 27 is, of course, totally ours. But how do we glimpse it, how do we comprehend it?

Be still with this Gospel, and allow words or phrases to sink below the level of your mind and reveal meanings in your heart.

Many of the cities of southern Europe – Avignon is a good example – are still surrounded by huge walls and massive fortified gates, built so that the citizens could decide to whom they would or would not allow entry.

Learning to pray is learning to be the gatekeeper of your own soul.

Jesus said, 'Do not let your hearts be troubled.' Do not allow it. Anxieties that threaten do not need to rampage through us wreaking the uniquely personal brand of havoc that each of us will know so despairingly well. Steadfastly we learn to practise the art of gatekeeping, refusing entry to that which troubles and haunts.

And then we attend to One who, astonishingly, has been there all along, who has made his 'home' but been ignored . . . and yet ever waits for our belonging.

The Moor

It was like a church to me.
I entered it on soft foot.
Breath held like a cap in the hand.
It was quiet.
What God was there made himself felt,
Not listened to, in clean colours
That brought a moistening of the eye,
In movement of the wind over grass.

There were no prayers said. But stillness
Of the heart's passions – that was praise
Enough; and the mind's cession
Of its kingdom. I walked on,
Simple and poor, while the air crumbled
And broke on me generously as bread.

R. S. Thomas [60]

111

Easter 7

Stilling and Centring

Take time to be still. Use a phrase from the psalm, or a word or phrase you have chosen, or follow your own path into stillness and adoration.

Psalm 63:4   *I will bless you as long as I live*
                  and lift up my hands in your name.

Offering

Offer your day that you may go on 'blessing' God, and may be a blessing to others you meet. Offer them and those places and people who intimidate you – where it is difficult to 'bless' God.

Reflecting

Reflect on John 17:20-26.

These words are part of the high priestly prayer of Jesus, which is the climax of the central section of John's Gospel (chapters 12-17). They express more fully the theme of 'innerness' touched on last week, pressing home how the inner life of Jesus Christ in the heart of the believer spells the end of all egoism so that those who dwell deeply 'in him' are indeed 'all one'.

Allow the words of his prayer to even become the words of your prayer.

As regards the denominations, Christians are not one. And may never be.

As regards belief amongst the faiths, huge differences persist, and will remain.

But there is a hidden underground path to the unity we seek that sometimes seems as far away as ever, as the doctrines and concepts go on dividing us. It is to learn to be still together – and in interior silence to name together the holy name of God, and in the experience of adoration to wake up to the illusion of separateness.

The deepest level of communication is not communication, but communion. It is wordless. It is beyond words . . . Not that we discover a new unity. We discover an older unity. My dear friends, we are already one. But we imagine that we are not. What we have to recover is our original unity. What we have to be is what we are.

Thomas Merton [61]

Pentecost

Stilling and Centring

Take time to be still. Use a phrase from the psalm, or a word or phrase you have chosen, or follow your own path into stillness and adoration.

Psalm 104:34   *I will sing to the Lord as long as I live;*
                 I will praise my God while I have my being.

Offering

In this week of the birthday of the Church, offer your concerns for the whole life of your church community and the wider church of God. Offer your day.

Reflecting

As you have time during the week reflect on John 14:8-17.

With his frustrated outburst: 'Lord show us the Father and then we shall be satisfied . . .', Philip precisely echoes our persistent sense that though we may well be stalwart members of the Church, we often feel far away from an inner experience of the Life of God that would silence our agitated and restless souls.

The response of Jesus: 'Do you not believe . . .', in which the word 'believe' occurs four times, poses the challenge of finding its inner meaning. How do we take the question of God out of the head where it will always struggle with doubt, and lay it down as the foundation stone of the heart so that it becomes the ground and support of all we are?

Let the phrases of this Gospel take you further into your own experience of what it means to 'believe'.

So much faith is backward looking, like digging out old photographs from the attic; a clutching at snapshots and searching for the glow of comfort from a romanticised past.

At Pentecost the world shakes, the verbs turn, the present lives; and a future, free from old and weary repetitions, becomes possible.

Now with you . . . will be in you. New meanings emerge. New discoveries are being made. New communities are born. New behaviour is practised. New worlds of truth and understanding and beauty are given.

We, both material for the working, and the stumbling apprentices . . . he, the disturbing Creator.

Abbot Lot came to Abbot Joseph and said: Father, according as I am able, I keep my little rule, and my little fast, my prayer, meditation and contemplative silence; and according as I am able I strive to cleanse my heart of thoughts: now what more should I do? The elder rose up in reply and stretched out his hands to heaven, and his fingers became like ten lamps of fire. He said: Why not be totally changed into fire?

Sayings of the Desert Fathers [62]

Trinity

Stilling and Centring

Take time to be still. Use a phrase from the psalm, or a word or phrase you have chosen, or follow your own path into stillness and adoration.

Psalm 63:8 *My soul clings to you;*
your right hand holds me fast.

Offering

In this week of Trinity Sunday as you emerge from your silence, offer your relationships with those who are closest to you. Offer them in their needs, and your time with them. Offer your day and your concerns.

Reflecting

As you have time during the week reflect on John 16:12-15.

In this short passage John deftly outlines the mysterious interrelatedness of the life of the Trinity. Jesus Christ, who has everything of the Father, is the centre of the Gospel. The Spirit is the One who 'declares' what is 'of' Jesus Christ. This declaring is not the shouting of a strident voice trying to persuade, but the silent inner pressing home of the knowledge of belonging to God, which shows itself in the self-authenticating truth of lives that are whole. That is the gift of Jesus Christ to receptive hearts – and to a lost world.

When you have found some stillness ask yourself what the phrases of this passage mean to you.

If we are to find solutions to our own problems or those of the world, we have to learn to be ignorant – to live openly, in trust, without knowing.

To a world obsessed with knowledge and starved of wisdom it is a strange and difficult way. The temptation is to force answers which, because they have not emerged from hearts that have waited and 'seen', don't fit.

To pray is to learn not to 'know' but to have the courage to wait until, led 'into all the truth', the perception dawns of simply the next step to be taken.

It is the fruit of a still and focused heart that has trusted enough simply to attend.

Like the inner of two bonded strips in a thermostat, the self curls against him and presses. The need for 'I' to have its 'thou', something other than ourselves yet sharing our subjectivity . . . survives all embarrassment, all silences . . . The sensation of silence cannot be helped; a loud and evident God would be a bully, an insecure tyrant . . . instead of, as he is, a bottomless encouragement to our faltering and frightened being.

John Updike [63]

Sunday between 29 May and 4 June
(if after Trinity)

Stilling and Centring

Take time to be still. Use a phrase from the psalm, or a word or phrase you have chosen, or follow your own path into stillness and adoration.

Psalm 96:9   *Worship the Lord in the beauty of holiness;*
let the whole earth stand in awe of him.

Offering

Offer your day – that you may learn to 'stand in awe of' and be aware of the Presence and Mystery of God. Offer those whom you will meet that your relationships together may be marked by profound respect.

Reflecting

As you have time during the week reflect on Luke 7:1b-10.

The focus in this passage is on the character and faith of this unnamed centurion, whom Jesus is 'amazed' at. It is not difficult to see why. This centurion: a) loves a people who are not his own; b) values a religion that is not his own; c) cares about his slave; d) is humble and self-effacing, not wishing 'to trouble' Jesus further; and e) is very conscious of his own shortcomings. He believes that Jesus has the authority of God, and he simply cries to him for help.

As you reflect on this passage try measuring yourself against this list of qualities. Let the passage take you into reflection on your own spirituality.

The seed-bed for genuine humility in a person is, paradoxically, a strong sense of self-worth. 'I am not worthy' and 'I do not presume to come' only make sense with an 'I' strong enough to face up to, and not be overrun by, its own weakness and moral failure.

Before we bow down we must learn to stand up.

Much traditional spirituality is far too fond of self-abasement, leading to a phoney humility that contains within it a kind of perverse pride. By contrast, learning to pray is learning to receive, before all else, God's unconditional 'Yes' to who I am. It means, each new day, coming into the light of Love and receiving the greeting of Love which, in my mock humility, I may find very difficult to accept.

But the more we receive this Yes, and discover our strength and our glory, the more we find how deeply flawed, compromised and damaged our lives are.

And then our cry is real – 'Lord have mercy upon me . . . I am *not* worthy . . .'

The first degree of humility consists in always keeping present in the mind the fear of God and absolutely avoiding forgetfulness of it.

The rule of Benedict of Nursia [64]

Sunday between 5 and 11 June
(if after Trinity)

Stilling and Centring

Take time to be still. Use a phrase from the psalm, or a word or phrase you have chosen, or follow your own path into stillness and adoration.

Psalm 30:1 *I will exalt you, O Lord,*
because you have lifted me up.

Offering

Offer your day – that there may be kept alive within you a deep sense of gratitude – of well-being for what you have received. Offer those whom you will meet and be grateful for them. Offer any concerns on your mind.

Reflecting

During the week reflect on Luke 7:11-17.

This picture of a meeting between anguished human grief and Divine power is painted in colours of the sharpest contrast. The grief, loss, hopelessness and insecurity of the mother surrounded by the large grieving crowd, contrasts powerfully with the compassion, authority, and stillness of Jesus, and the new life and reuniting that he brings.

As you allow your imagination to work on the detail of this story let it illuminate your condition and need of grace.

From time to time, praying gets completely stuck. We arrive at our prayer time and feel nothing. If we can reflect at all, we may become aware of a kind of 'deadening' process that has been creeping upon us for some time. Like the son in the story we see that more and more we are just being carried along . . . simply doing the next thing that has to be done, our lives increasingly unresponsive, functional, and dead.

At the heart of the story, Jesus touches the bier and the bearers stand still.

Resisting the compulsion to go on, and bringing our drivenness into stillness is a precondition for any change. Realising how cold, hard and frozen we are is very uncomfortable. Sometimes others have to tell us.

But if we can stop, breathe slowly, and begin to say again and again out of the depths of a frozen heart, 'Lord have mercy upon me . . .', the beginnings of resurrection become possible.

Margaret Miles of the Harvard Divinity School has discussed the original meaning of Christian holiness. She points out that before Christian faith was thought of as knowledge or commitment or community, it was lived as an orientation to the source of life; it was lived as a conversion to full vitality from the deadness of secular culture. Miles claims that being truly alive for the first Christians was not the opposite of physical death, but the opposite of the death of the human heart: coldness, dullness, failure to respond, an obtuse spirit.

Robert E. Kennedy [65]

Sunday between 12 and 18 June
(if after Trinity)

Stilling and Centring

Take time to be still. Either use a phrase from the psalm, or a word or phrase you have chosen, or follow your own path into stillness and adoration.

Psalm 5:8   *Lead me, O Lord, in your righteousness,*
                make your way straight before me.

Offering

Offer the detail of your life this day and this week – that in small and large ways, and in ways you are entirely unaware of, your life may reveal something of the life and grace of God.

Reflecting

During the week reflect on Luke 7:36-8:3.

Another story of vivid contrast: the despised woman who loves extravagantly as against the righteous Pharisee who does not.

At the heart of it is a great outpouring of adoration and gratitude as the woman knows with a knowledge too deep for words that by this man, if by no other, she is valued, accepted, and even forgiven.

Give yourself time to transpose the meanings that you find in the passage into your situation.

There are many obstacles standing in the way of the integration we seek.

Sometimes, even in the most apparently balanced of minds, there lurks a half-conscious dread of what might emerge from the depths of the psyche to haunt and accuse if silence really had a chance. So we keep busy, insulated from any extended silence or the emptiness of a long retreat. And we remain shallow people.

Courage is necessary: courage to go into stillness; courage to discover how, as you focus mind and heart completely on the One who is both Lover and Beloved, the unnamed dread strangely disappears like damp fog evaporating before a rising sun. And you find that the place of silence becomes, against all expectation, a place of unexpected and liberating delight.

It is the power of acceptance overcoming fear, the illusion of dread, again and again.

Adoration, then, on the one hand is a bowing in awe before the divine mystery which we contemplate like one standing before an infinite sea of love . . . On the other hand adoration is something we grow into through the daily slog of discipline . . . a matter of patience, discipline, of the repeated small gesture which we hope will slowly enlarge the capacity of the heart.

Terry Tastard [66]

Sunday between 19 and 25 June

Stilling and Centring

Take time to be still. Use a phrase from the psalm, or a word or phrase you have chosen, or follow your own path into stillness and adoration.

Psalm 42:7   *Put your trust in God,*
for I will yet give thanks to him
who is the help of my countenance and my God.

Offering

Offer your day and your concerns that throughout the day your sense of actively trusting may be kept alive. Offer all those who find it hard to trust.

Reflecting

During the week reflect on Luke 8:26-39.

Couched in the common understandings of the time – that mental illness was a result of demon possession – this story seems at first glance alien and frightening to modern ears. And yet is it so strange? Even for the supposedly 'normal', let alone those who suffer the hell of mental illness, the experience of being overwhelmed or 'invaded' by irrational fears and anxieties is very commonplace. Our everyday language gives us away: 'I wasn't myself' we say, or 'I don't know what got into me'.

It is a rare person who has not sensed the terrifying prospect of what it is to be out of control, who has not at some point glimpsed into the abyss of mental chaos, or has not simply felt at war internally.

It is a searching story. Be still, and in the confidence of the Love of God allow the passage to connect with your experience.

We can be many people. At first pliable and adaptable, we mould identities around ourselves like a child with Plasticine or a potter with clay. And the shaping goes on and on until the pot becomes, over time, fired by pain. Fixed and glazed, we find we are formed into someone immovable, brittle, hard-edged.

To pray is to begin the long task of unlearning and forgetting – the fixed responses painfully shaped, the tired hand-me-down scripts, the contoured masks, the next word that I always say.

Bathed in the gaze of a Love that waits for ever, we find hidden beneath the debris of our years an Original Face whom from time to time we may have remembered but, with the lights glaring upon us, we had forgotten.

There must always be two kinds of art, escape art, for man needs escape as he needs food and deep sleep, and parable art, the art which shall teach man to unlearn hatred and learn love . . .

W. H. Auden

. . . the ultimate knowledge, the love-knowledge of the Trinity, takes hold of us by grace alone. We prepare for it by a stripping away of our being until we become nothing but expectation. In Simone Weil's admittedly approximate expression, we must 'de-create' ourselves, and descend . . . to those luminous deep waters on which the Spirit breathes: to the waters of baptism, the waters of creation. Then the Spirit comes as he came upon Mary and the person is created afresh in 'an ineffable peace and silence.'

Olivier Clément [67]

Sunday between 26 June and 2 July

Stilling and Centring

Take time to be still. Use a phrase from the psalm, or a word or phrase you have chosen, or follow your own path into stillness and adoration.

Psalm 16:11   *You will show me the path of life;*
in your presence there is fullness of joy.

Offering

Offer your day that you may not miss the opportunities given, the path of life that opens up when we may least expect it. Offer those whom you will spend time with this day, this week.

Reflecting

Reflect on Luke 9:51-62.

The note here is one of urgency, determination and a call for immediate decision. Luke tells us he 'set his face', implying an utterly single-minded purpose – the Life-giving reign of God before everything else. In the light of this dawning kingdom nothing else matters, not housing and comfort, not family obligations, not even the mourning of the dead. Everything pales into insignificance in the light of the kingdom that is here . . . now. Focus on that alone, and immediately, lest you miss it.

Let the urgent call to life that is at the heart of this passage resonate in your particular circumstances.

The New Testament may be good news, but it also contains a terrible warning – that it is perfectly possible to miss that news altogether.

Such is our preoccupation with laudable concerns – our security and comfort, our family obligations – that we may simply not see the moments we are offered, not hear the calls we are given. With our goals fixed and our routines time-honoured, we may just go sleepwalking on finally never to wake up at all.

If we are to respond to a new day that we don't yet see, we have 'to set our face'.

Praying is this 'setting', a focusing towards something infinitely beyond which may cost us everything, even as everything is transformed.

So be very careful how you spend your time. There is nothing more precious. In the twinkling of an eye heaven may be won or lost.

The Cloud of Unknowing [68]

We forget that God exists, that we can receive him at every moment; we ignore our neighbours; we lose the capacity for wonder; and we end up living like sleepwalkers.

Olivier Clément [69]

Sunday between 3 and 9 July

Stilling and Centring

Take time to be still. Use a phrase from the psalm, or a word or phrase you have chosen, or follow your own path into stillness and adoration.

Psalm 16:7   *I will bless the Lord who gives me counsel;*
my heart teaches me, night after night.

Offering

Offer your day and your week that you may remain grounded in the peace you have found, your heart resting in the Love of God. Offer any you know whose lives are particularly stressed, or who are carrying burdens too heavy for them.

Reflecting

During the week reflect on Luke 10:1-11, 16-20.

This vivid account of the sending out of the seventy brims with confident certainty in the triumph of God which leads to peace. The first words they are to say, echoing Jesus' greeting after the resurrection, is 'Peace to this house.' At the end of the passage as they return flushed with 'success', they are again reminded that the source of any lasting joy or peace is nothing achieved, but that 'their names are written in heaven' and they belong to God.

To go out from peace in confident trust; to proclaim peace come what may; to return and be grounded again in the belonging from which all peace comes – this is the daily rhythm of the life of faith.

In a 'doing' rather than a 'being' culture, 'achievement' and 'success' are all and the threat of possible failure looms disproportionately large casting deep, fearful shadows. Congratulations are short-lived and come with strings attached. Another 'target' is set. The ratchet of strain is increased.

Not much rest; not much 'peace'.

To pray is to swim into a deeper stream. It's hard work but healing as we slowly arrive again, and remember . . . from whom we go out . . . to whom we return . . . and in whom we belong.

Un penseur moderne a imagine l'homme moderne comme un homme qui est sorti de sa maison et qui a perdu la cle pour y rentrer.
(A modern thinker has imagined modern man as someone who is outside his own house and has lost the key to get back in.)

From the prayer to Saint Benedict in the
crypt of the monastery of S. Benoit sur Loire

Every human heart is a hermitage if we care to enter and find ourselves there in union with all.

Laurence Freeman [70]

Sunday between 10 and 16 July

Stilling and Centring

Take time to be still. Use a phrase from the psalm, or a word or phrase you have chosen, or follow your own path into stillness and adoration.

Psalm 25:3   *Show me your ways, O Lord*
            and teach me your paths.

Offering

Offer yourself for the day ahead that you may remain alert to the Mystery of Another Life in and through you.

Reflecting

During the week reflect on Luke 10:25-37.

Another vivid contrast! The spontaneous compassion, and spiritual and psychological freedom of the Samaritan is set against the fear and cold-hearted disdain of the priest and Levite passing by; and by implication, the self-justifying lawyer who asks the question.

But we are all judged by this story. It measures the distance between us and what Jesus of Nazareth called 'Life'.

Don't let familiarity dull you to the meanings hidden in this passage. Read it slowly, let it go deep.

To pray is to learn how not to fear and to become compassionate.

Of course it is impossible for human beings to do this. Left to ourselves we are to a greater or lesser degree always on guard, watchfully patrolling the boundaries of the ego, alert to any threat, ever ready to defend.

Real compassion? We cannot do it.

That's why the only way forward is to leave ourselves entirely behind . . . and to step into the life of Another.

It seems absurd. But this is what praying is about.

It is no longer I who live but Christ who lives in me.

Paul of Tarsus [71]

Sunday between 17 and 23 July

Stilling and Centring

Take time to be still. Use a phrase from the psalm, or a word or phrase you have chosen, or follow your own path into stillness and adoration.

Psalm 63:5   *My soul is content: as with marrow and fatness,*
and my mouth praises you with joyful lips.

Offering

Offer your day and all whom you will meet and all that you will do. Offer those whom you know whose lives seem to be very distracted.

Reflecting

During the week reflect on Luke 10:38-42.

The classic Gospel of the contemplative life, with its contrast between Martha distracted by many tasks, and Mary focused on one.

The Greek word 'periespato' translated here as 'distracted' literally means 'to draw off from around', i.e. she responded to whatever stimulus, demand, or pressure was around. And so she was pulled, this way and that, fretful, unfocused.

'Martha, Martha,' the name is called more than once to one who doesn't hear.

Be aware of your own tendency to 'draw off from around' as you reflect on this passage. We need to draw the water of life from somewhere deeper.

On my bookshelves I have a book with the intriguing title: 'All you love is need'. The author describes a society in which relationships are increasingly defined by 'need'; and where the capacity to love – that is to give of oneself to another person without any calculation – is diminishing. The result is a desert in our common life in which more and more people are thirsty and desperate for that which is so badly needed in fractured and hurt lives, but never comes.

So we become needs-driven – with disastrous results.

What we most need is an oasis, a hidden wellspring from which we may 'draw off' that which alone can end this kind of dereliction . . . and will set us free to give.

It is the only thing needed.

Do not let it be distracted or torn this way or that by thoughts. Let it become, I say, completely a waiting upon Christ.

Pseudo-Macarius [72]

While the ego scatters our attention in a myriad of directions, inwardly the heart always looks towards God. Repeating His name, we turn from the many to the one.

Llewellyn Vaughan-Lee [73]

Sunday between 24 and 30 July

Stilling and Centring

Take time to be still. Use a phrase from the psalm, or a word or phrase you have chosen, or follow your own path into stillness and adoration.

Psalm 16:8   *I have set the Lord always before me;*
because he is at my right hand I shall not fall.

Offering

Offer your day that in all that you face you may remember the Life of God within you. Offer those you will be with this day, this week.

Reflecting

During the week reflect on Luke 11:1-13.

Beyond the prayer itself, the nub of this passage is persistence. The three-fold imperative: 'to ask', 'to search' and 'to find' underline that the fullness of the life of God cannot just be 'given'. That would be to obliterate human freedom, and to destroy that understanding which is at the heart of the Judaeo-Christian revelation that God is both the Ground of our being and also paradoxically somehow Other to us such that we may know him in the phrase made famous by Martin Buber as 'I to Thou.'

One way to reflect on and to pray this passage would be to take one phrase from the Lord's Prayer each day, and repeat it, slowly searching for the meanings hidden within it – and hidden in you.

134

The 'name' of God is not some kind of label to 'describe' the Divine; a ludicrous idea.

The Name is the Presence itself.

To hold this name as holy – or 'hallow' it – the first petition . . . is to enter into the power of Being, and, adoring, for a longed-for moment to be found.

It is, in fact, written that 'No one can say "Jesus is Lord" except by the Holy Spirit' (1 Corinthians 12:3) . . . Those who meditate on this holy and glorious Name continually in the depths of their heart can see also the light of their own spirit. For if it is enter-tained with great care by the mind, the Name with intense emotion destroys all the impurities that cover the surface of the soul.

Diadochus of Photike [74]

Sunday between 31 July and 6 August

Stilling and Centring

Take time to be still. Use a phrase from the psalm, or a word or phrase you have chosen, or follow your own path into stillness and adoration.

Psalm 66:7-8 *Bless our God . . . who holds our souls in life,*
and will not allow our feet to slip.

Offering

Offer your day confident in the freedom that you can and will make mistakes as you take the risks of faith, and that it is all right. Our feet will not be allowed ultimately to slip. Offer your work and your plans for this day and the time ahead.

Reflecting

During the week reflect on Luke 12:13-21.

This is an extraordinarily contemporary parable with its explicit warning against 'all kinds of greed', and the reminder that life is a dynamic process either of growth and change towards wisdom, love and the capacity for greater sacrifice and prayerfulness, or of decline, decay and disintegration as greed and desire is succumbed to, with the possibility that the person may eventually be entirely overrun.

Reflect on it slowly. Let it act as both warning and encouragement.

Every day we are under subtle, artful pressure – seductive images, beguiling fantasies, and suggestive portrayals of how I might be and who I *could* be play on insecurities . . . cajoling, suggesting.

To pray is to guard an island of time where there is absolutely nothing to do . . . but wait . . . until out of the blank space left behind as the fantasies dissolve . . . a still Life is given.

I am. Again.

And God returns to a place he never left.

'Rich towards God' – from nothing.

It is an indelible principle of eternal truth, that practice and exercise is the life of all. Should God give you worlds, and laws, and treasures, and worlds upon worlds and himself also in the divinest manor, if you will be lazy, and not meditate, you lose all. The soul is made for action, and cannot rest till it be employed. Idleness is its rust. Unless it will up and think and taste and see, all is in vain.

Thomas Traherne [75]

. . . be as eager not to possess as people usually are to possess.

Diadochus of Photike [76]

Sunday between 7 and 13 August

Stilling and Centring

Take time to be still. Use a phrase from the psalm, or a word or phrase you have chosen, or follow your own path into stillness and adoration.

Psalm 33:20   *Our soul waits for the Lord;*
he is our help and our shield.

Offering

Offer your day that you may be ready for the unexpected. Offer all whom you will meet and spend time with.

Reflecting

During the week reflect on Luke 12:32-40.

There are two calls in this passage: to a radical detachment from all possessiveness and a consequent freedom from anxiety about what we may own; and to a disciplined alertness ready for the One who will break into our world at the most unexpected moments.

As you reflect on this passage and your own life, ask yourself, 'How am I responding to these calls in my particular circumstances?'

We are cocooned in an illusion which says that this world is all there is; and we, planning, calculating, targeting, implementing, assessing . . . control it.

Masters of all we survey – which is as far as the edge of the illusion.

The task of all true religion is to break out of this stifling cocoon, with its useless liturgies and its time spent alertly doing nothing . . .

. . . except waiting for Reality to dawn.

Much of what is done in this work called contemplation is training. Training the mind, the body, the self, for the time of ripening, to break through the sytems and the propaganda to see things as they really are.

Gregory Mayers [77]

Sunday between 14 and 20 August

Stilling and Centring

Take time to be still. Use a phrase from the psalm, or a word or phrase you have chosen, or follow your own path into stillness and adoration.

Psalm 33:22   *Let your loving-kindness, O Lord, be upon us,*
as we put our trust in you.

Offering

Offer yourself that you may be able to see what is going on in you and around you. This day and this week, have the eyes to see, the ears to listen, the heart to understand, and the courage to act.

Reflecting

During the week reflect on Luke 12:49-56.

However we interpret this complex passage, written out of the life experience of the early Church where there was division and awful persecution, we can at least hear in it a powerful note of divine frustration with our unresponsiveness and deadness.

It is a call to wake out of the sleep of our death-dealing ways, and live and love and face the confusion that this waking up will inevitably bring.

Don't be afraid to let your imagination work on this difficult passage. Allow time for meanings to emerge.

In reality the monk abandons the world only in order to listen more intently to the deepest and most neglected voices that proceed from its inner depth.

The American contemplative Thomas Merton became a hermit not because he wanted to hide away in his little cinder-block hut, but so that in the silence of the woods he might learn to listen, understand and *see*; and seeing, call softly to the world, 'turn and *look.*'

The hermit vocation exists, however undeveloped, in each one of us. Without it the world, and us as part of it, just crashes on, blind, insensitive, wounding, hurting . . .

Why pray?

Simply in order to wake up, listen – and see.

The basic command of religion is not 'do this!' or 'do that!' but simply 'look!'

Philip Toynbee [78]

Sunday between 21 and 27 August

Stilling and Centring

Take time to be still. Use a phrase from the psalm, or a word or phrase you have chosen, or follow your own path into stillness and adoration.

Psalm 112:4   *Light shines in the darkness for the upright.*
The righteous are merciful and full of compassion.

Offering

Offer your day, your week, that the life of Christ may live in you and through you in all that you must do. Offer all whom you will meet this day, and those you know who especially need the compassion of Christ.

Reflecting

During the week reflect on Luke 13:10-17.

This passage is a celebration of a Gospel which restores human strength and dignity. The woman stands up 'straight'. Here is the hope that life can be released from the complexities of evil which bear down upon us, and bend and break human beings. In and through this Christ, God's life bursts through the fixed deadness of human routines symbolised by the over-prescriptive Sabbath observance.

There is a new creation under way – even *now*.

Pray this passage, slowly, gently . . . seeking meanings for yourself, and for others.

As a young curate I remember struggling to help a woman crippled by fear; in her heart a child's terror of a god who eternally punishes. She was unable to 'stand up straight'.

To hold to the name of Christ as all-embracing love in that kind of devastated inner landscape requires a leap of courage – a daring to stand against all that the inner child believes to be true.

But if, with help and a kind of naked faith that has no ground of experience to tread upon, a foothold can nevertheless be gained and held against the flood of continuing inner condemnation; and if love can be believed in despite everything that is felt, the fears will slowly die, becoming no more real than old ghosts of a winter past.

For we have learnt to look elsewhere, and bathed in the spring light of an acceptance at last believed in . . .

. . . to stand.

We make our prayer standing upright on the first day of the week (Sunday) . . . it is not only because, being risen with Christ and being bound to seek the things that are above, we are reminding ourselves, by standing upright on the day consecrated to the resurrection, of the grace that has been given to us, but it is also because this day is in some way an image of the age to come . . . This day is, in fact, also the eighth day and it symbolises the fullness that will follow the present time, the day that never closes . . . the age that will never come to an end . . . It is therefore necessary that the Church should bring up her children to pray standing upright on this day, so that with a continual reminder of life without end we should not forget to make ready our food for the journey . . . The upright posture . . . makes our soul, so to speak, emigrate from the land of the present to that of the future.

Basil of Caesarea [79]

Sunday between 28 Aug and 3 Sept

Stilling and Centring

Take time to be still. Use a phrase from the psalm, or a word or phrase you have chosen, or follow your own path into stillness and adoration.

Psalm 103:1   *Bless the Lord, O my soul*
and all that is within me bless his holy name.

Offering

Offer your day and all that you are to do; and offer yourself that you may know, beyond all doubt, your own infinite worth. You bear within you the Image of God.

Reflecting

During the week reflect on Luke 14:1, 7-14.

It is hard for the modern western reader, unfamiliar with traditions of honour and shame that are still powerful in Middle Eastern cultures, to appreciate the depth of meaning in this passage. But the need for recognition from others, and the thirst for public accolade is universal and all too familiar.

Reflect on the passage slowly. Let it speak to your situation, to your character.

We cannot escape our need and our searching for a place to be honoured.

We either choose it in public, inflate ourselves, push others out, cause resentment, and run the risk of humiliation; or we choose it in private, going to the place where a more secret 'honouring' frees us.

Then we may sit high or low.

It no longer matters.

What is this mystery concerning my condition? I received the image of God and did not know how to keep it.

Gregory Nazianzen [80]

It is the breath of God that you breathe – and you are unaware of it.

Theophilus of Antioch [81]

145

Sunday between 4 and 10 September

Stilling and Centring

Take time to be still. Use a phrase from the psalm, or a word or phrase you have chosen, or follow your own path into stillness and adoration.

Psalm 1:3   *They are like trees planted by streams of water,*
bearing fruit in due season
with leaves that do not wither.

Offering

Offer your life for this coming day that you may be alert to the Mystery of God within and around you and that your actions and words may not simply be the noise of your ego-self, but emerge from somewhere deeper within you.

Reflecting

Reflect on Luke 14:25-33.

With phrases like 'hate father and mother' and 'give up all your possessions', this is a very difficult passage; but hugely liberating, even if we can only glimpse what it means. At its heart is the call to put Jesus Christ before everything else, setting us free to enjoy everything else – as gift.

So obsessed are we with possession it is very difficult to understand this, let alone live it. It is a freedom that comes from a stance of very radical 'detachment' – the other side of a cross. If we cannot grasp all that is meant, we can make small and significant steps in the direction of handing over, of freeing, as we learn to utter from the depths of our heart again and again: 'Jesus Christ is Lord.'

As you focus on worship, adoration and thanksgiving, let this passage go deeply into your soul. Work at it, until you find meanings.

It is astonishing that Christianity should ever be popular, when at its fullest it is a yielding up, a handing over and a dying – a dying to all my plans and projects, a giving up of all that I possess – a total end to the idea of me as separate autonomous individual.

In PR terms it is disastrous, and yet extraordinarily, it has flowered. Perhaps we humans have intuitively sensed that this is what is needed to transform us – a surrender.

Learning to say 'Jesus Christ is Lord' is, every day, a small dying. And then after we have begun to mean it, a waiting – which always follows death, until we begin to gain a sense that what has so painfully been handed over is coming back . . . a hundredfold.

. . . to fully hear the word of the cross is more than a simple assent to the teaching that Christ died for our sins. It means to be nailed to the cross with Christ so that the ego-self is no longer the principle of our deepest actions which now proceed from Christ living in us.

Robert E. Kennedy [82]

Sunday between 11 and 17 September

Stilling and Centring

Take time to be still. Use a phrase from the psalm, or a word or phrase you have chosen, or follow your own path into stillness and adoration.

Psalm 51:1 *Have mercy on me O God,*
according to your loving-kindness;
in your great compassion blot out my offences.

Offering

Offer your life for the coming day or week that you may not become 'lost' in your own egoism, your fears and self-obsession, but remain 'found' and free in the Love of God. Offer any who especially need your prayers for this day.

Reflecting

During the week reflect on Luke 15:1-10.

The lost sheep, the lost coin . . . the first two of the three losing and finding stories in Luke, chapter 15.

Give time for your imagination to work into the fabric of these stories. Explore the meanings that are hidden there and connect them with your life and experience.

Our need to pray may grow out of very positive experiences – wonder at a stunning scene of natural beauty, thankfulness for the good things life has given us, or a sudden gesture of kindness.

But it may well be that a deeper experience of prayer will have its roots in very negative things – our frustration and anger, our restlessness, agitation, or anguish.

It is always a moment of hope when, instead of rampaging around hurting others because we are hurting ourselves, it somehow dawns upon us that the only way out of the hell we are causing is to go in search of something that is lost . . .

Ourselves . . .

. . . whom only the silence and mercy of God can find.

It was not outside but in her house that the woman who had lost her silver coin found it again. She had lighted the lamp and swept out the house, and it was there that she found her silver coin. For your part, if you light your 'lamp' . . . if you 'see light in his light', you will find the silver coin in you. For the image of the heavenly king is in you . . . (God) does not imprint this image on the outside but within . . . It could not be seen in you as long as your house was dirty, full of refuse and rubbish . . .

Origen [83]

Sunday between 18 and 24 September

Stilling and Centring

Take time to be still. Use a phrase from the psalm, or a word or phrase you have chosen, or follow your own path into stillness and adoration.

Psalm 91:1   *He who dwells in the shelter of the Most High,*
abides under the shadow of the Almighty.

Offering

Offer your day and all whom you will meet that in all the circumstances you face and the needs you will encounter, in yourself and others, you may go on dwelling 'in the shelter of the Most High' . . . abiding 'under the shadow'.

Reflecting

During the week reflect on Luke 16:1-13.

This passage bristles with difficulties of interpretation. For example, it seems very strange that the master 'commended' the dishonest manager when the manager had defrauded him of a lot of money. And then the various sentences don't seem to connect: we are told 'to make friends by means of dishonest wealth', and then the next sentence says 'whoever is faithful in very little is also faithful in much'. It is complex, and the reader could usefully consult a good commentary.

For the purposes of reflecting on and praying this gospel don't worry too much about the inconsistencies; just let the texts which may well have become disconnected from one another in the tradition of the early Church, awaken meanings in you.

Focus slowly on different sentences in the passage, finding what understandings are awakened in you and how it connects with your experience.

We tend to think that the things we own, or dream of owning, are mere things, just objects. We don't recognise their subtle power, the way they can 'own' us . . . capturing minds, exciting imaginations, stoking up longings.

Before we know it, we have 'yielded them our allegiance'.

That is why the saints in all traditions stress the need to give up everything – all possessions. They know what a trap things can be, the insidious way that even while we think we are enjoying them, they are in fact quietly, and with our entire complicity, robbing us of ourselves.

To pray is to focus on no thing. Nothing.

A strange and paradoxical path – to everything.

In order to have pleasure in everything
Desire to have pleasure in nothing.
In order to arrive at possessing everything
Desire to possess nothing.
In order to arrive at being everything
Desire to be nothing.
In order to arrive at knowing everything
Desire to know nothing.

St John of the Cross [84]

Sunday between 25 Sept and 1 Oct

Stilling and Centring

Take time to be still. Use a phrase from the psalm, or a word or phrase you have chosen, or follow your own path into stillness and adoration.

Psalm 91:4   *He shall cover you with his pinions,*
and you shall find refuge under his wings;
his faithfulness shall be a shield and buckler.

Offering

Offer the coming day or week – and offer all those who are exposed to the cruelties and injustices of the world. Offer your efforts to respond, with others, to injustice.

Reflecting

During the week reflect on Luke 16:19-31.

Another difficult passage: briefly, it would seem that the parable may well have been a Jewish version of an old Egyptian folk-tale and, 'the details of conditions in the world of the dead are merely a reflection of current popular notions and ought not to be taken as data of revelation.' *(See reference to Beare below, p. 182.)*

Because of its difficulties, one commentator believes that 'the whole peri-cope is the construction of some early Christian teacher; there is little to confirm its attribution to Jesus himself.' *(F. W. Beare, The Earliest Records of Jesus, Blackwell, Oxford.)*

Whether or not this is true, the central ideas – injustice, disregard for the suffering of others, gross self-indulgence, the need for repentance – are central to Christian teaching and need to act upon us in terms of corrective and warning.

A degree of fasting and self-denial has always been part of any authentic spiritual life.

To set one's face for limited periods of time against the subtle addictions of food, and learn to wait only for the Bread of Life, is one small step towards freedom . . .

. . . and one small response to the outrage of a world divided between obesity and hunger.

God is the beggar knocking at the door of our soul asking for love.

Olivier Clément [85]

Sunday between 2 and 8 October

Stilling and Centring

Take time to be still. Use a phrase from the psalm, or a word or phrase you have chosen, or follow your own path into stillness and adoration.

Psalm 37:4   *Take delight in the Lord*
and he shall give you your heart's desire.

Offering

Offer those you will be with this day – what is your 'heart's desire' for them? Offer yourself that you may keep a sense of 'delight' in who you meet, in what you discover this day, and this week.

Reflecting

During the week reflect on Luke 17:5-10.

The story of the 'worthless slaves' should not be pressed too far as indicating God's attitude to us. (Jesus usually taught that our relationship to God was like a Father to a son rather than a master to a slave.) The point of the story is a warning against presuming that any merit or goodness can establish a claim on God as of right. All is of grace – free and unmerited.

It is worth noting that in fact Christ 'acts' as slave to us – getting down on his knees with a basin of water and washing feet.

Take time to explore any connections between the passage and your life.

'We are worthless slaves' . . . Some people find the words of the prayer of humble access – 'We do not presume' . . . 'We are not worthy . . .', decidedly unhealthy. To them it smacks too much of a grovelling demeanour of low self-esteem all too common amongst church people.

We need to get to the heart of our true unworthiness – which is not to sufficiently love and respect ourselves and others, created as we are in God's image.

And then we can say, 'Lord have mercy upon me – I am not worthy because I refuse to believe in who I really am.'

The word 'Eleison', meaning 'have mercy', is the same root as 'eleion' meaning oil . . . the oil of gladness.

. . . while we were . . . desiring intensely to attain to this sovereign Wisdom we touched it slightly for a whole heartbeat.

Augustine of Hippo [86]

Sunday between 9 and 15 October

Stilling and Centring

Take time to be still. Use a phrase from the psalm, or a word or phrase you have chosen, or follow your own path into stillness and adoration.

Psalm 111:1   *Alleluia!*
I will give thanks to the Lord with my whole heart,
in the assembly of the upright, in the congregation.

Offering

Offer your day that you may have a renewed sense of thanksgiving and trust in the providence of God every step of the way, that resources for coping will be found as you need them. Offer those with whom you will spend this day, and this week.

Reflecting

During the week reflect on Luke 17:11-19.

A beautiful account of healing with the explosive punch-line: 'And he was a Samaritan', which is difficult for us to appreciate but is in one sense the centre of the whole story.

The other punch-line – 'your faith has made you well' – raises the question, 'How is this faith that makes well, to be exercised?' In particular, how are we to exercise it within the practice and discipline of praying?

This story lead very naturally into prayer and adoration. Reflect on the texts slowly and repetitively, letting them go deeper and deeper into you, connecting with your experience.

One of the difficulties of interpreting the New Testament stories is that they can seem like magic with healings done in a flash, whereas we know that the journey of clearing out the muddle and havoc of our inner lives takes a lifetime.

Learning to patiently and repeatedly cry from our depths, 'Jesus, Master, have mercy on us', is to step onto this lifelong Way . . .

. . . remembering that the healing happened 'as they went'.

There is in each of us a Self that lies deeper than our conscious ego, that still point of your being where you are most truly you, so that the journey of prayer is largely a journey inwards. Not that prayer is self-analysis. Quite the reverse: it is a way of becoming detached, of escaping at least momentarily from the constant clamour of the self. It is the way we begin to shift the centre of living from self-consciousness to self-surrender.

Michael Mayne [87]

Sunday between 16 and 22 October

Stilling and Centring

Take time to be still. Use a phrase from the psalm, or a word or phrase you have chosen, or follow your own path into stillness and adoration.

Psalm 121:8 *The Lord shall watch over your going out*
and your coming in,
from this time forth for evermore.

Offering

Offer your day that you may somehow remain a praying person throughout the day, still alert to the Mystery of God amidst all your business. Offer any you know whose faith is being severely tested, or who are in grief, or who are in some way, perhaps without words, 'crying to him day and night . . .'

Reflecting

During the week reflect on Luke 18:1-8.

This parable may have come from a period of severe persecution in the early Church, a time when his chosen ones in their suffering were 'crying to him day and night.'

The message of the parable is in the contrast between the character of the arrogant uncaring judge, and the character of God – ever merciful and ever just, who always hears and loves and is answering even though we cannot see it.

Pray the passage through the week for yourself and others.

There will come times of awful loss and pain when all we can do is sit in the dark and name the name of the One who died . . . but yet lives . . .

. . . and who 'keeps' the heart which we have lost.

Our efforts might seem ineffective, and they might seem to disappear amid the routines of our daily life, but this is as it should be. The salt hiding in the soup makes it more tasty. The yeast in the dough turns it into bread. The more hidden the practice becomes in our daily life, the more it disappears to where it can do its work.

Gregory Mayers [88]

Sunday between 23 and 29 October

Stilling and Centring

Take time to be still. Use a phrase from the psalm, or a word or phrase you have chosen, or follow your own path into stillness and adoration.

Psalm 119:103   *How sweet are your words to my taste;*
they are sweeter than honey to my mouth.

Offering

In the strength of the silence, and your awareness of the mercy and grace of God to you, offer your day, your love and your concern for others.

Reflecting

During the week reflect on Luke 18:9-14.

This is one of the gems of the New Testament taking us to the very heart of what authentic spirituality is about.

Let this passage connect deeply with you, judging and healing.

To repeat the Kyrie Eleison, 'Lord, have mercy . . . Lord have mercy', again and again is extraordinarily healing, and can gently open up a kind of inner door to the experience of God in the heart.

One simple phrase opens up the hugeness of our need, the extent of our longing, and as we persist with it, breaks down and demolishes all latent pride.

And as we learn to go on, mental gaze focused on nothing else, in what becomes a more and more profound cry, it pours in a consoling and uniting grace that, for a while, makes whole.

'Lord Jesus Christ, Son of God, have mercy on me . . .'

Say it again and again – the prayer of the pilgrim.

Kneeling

Moments of great calm,
Kneeling before an altar
Of wood in a stone church
In summer, waiting for the God
To speak; the air a staircase
For silence; the sun's light
Ringing me, as though I acted
A great role. And the audiences
Still; all that close throng
Of spirits waiting, as I,
For the message.
Prompt me, God;
But not yet. When I speak
Though it be you who speak
Through me, something is lost.
The meaning is in the waiting.

R. S. Thomas [89]

Dedication Festival
(which may be kept on the Last Sunday after Trinity)

Stilling and Centring

Take time to be still. Use a phrase from the psalm, or a word or phrase you have chosen, or follow your own path into stillness and adoration.

Psalm 84:1   *How dear to me is your dwelling, O Lord of hosts;*
my soul has a desire and longing
for the courts of the Lord;
my heart and my flesh rejoice in the living God.

Offering

Offer your day, and offer the priorities of your life – what really matters to you. Offer the extent of your 'longing for the courts of the Lord'.

Reflecting

During the week reflect on John 2:13-22.

This passage is ablaze with the consuming priority of Jesus of Nazareth – the love of his 'Father' before everything. To hold the name of God as holy, and to place that holy name back at the centre of the life of the nation, and of the human heart, was his passion.

Allow your imagination to work into this story and connect it with your experience and spirituality.

Sometimes the condition that we find ourselves in requires more than our occasional intermittent and dutiful efforts at a praying life which may be increasingly worn. Overrun by distractions, hasty and reactive – something sooner or later happens, perhaps a sharp upset in our personal lives, that makes us uncomfortably aware that a determined reordering and clearing out is essential. We need an assault on the chaotic territory of our heart where we increasingly feel there is little room for us to breathe, let alone pray.

A determined assault takes courage to plan. A retreat, time away alone, a holiday, a long talk with a trusted and wise friend – all of these are necessities in the recovery of any balanced life.

And then a more simple discipline is all that is needed to keep watch over a space reclaimed . . .

. . . for silence and God – again.

Silence is nothing else but waiting for God's Word and coming from God's Word with a blessing. But everybody knows that this is something that needs to be practised and learned, in these days when talkativeness prevails. Real silence, real stillness, really holding one's tongue comes only as the sober consequence of spiritual stillness.

But this stillness before the Word will exert its influence upon the whole day. If we have learned to be silent before the Word, we shall also learn to manage our silence and our speech during the day.

The silence of the Christian is listening silence, humble stillness, that may be interrupted at any time for the sake of humility.

Dietrich Bonhoeffer [90]

Fourth Sunday before Advent

Stilling and Centring

Take time to be still. Use a phrase from the psalm, or a word or phrase you have chosen, or follow your own path into stillness and adoration.

Psalm 27:7   *For in the day of trouble*
he shall keep me safe in his shelter;
he shall hide me in the secrecy of his dwelling
and set me high upon a rock.

Offering

Offer any problems, any 'trouble' that is bothering you. Offer your sense of being both hidden in a shelter, and high upon a rock. Offer your day, your week.

Reflecting

During the week reflect on Luke 19:1-10.

One of the very best of Luke's stories with its vivid image of the rich little tax collector in the undignified posture of scrambling up a tree because he wanted to *see*.

Allow yourself to acknowledge the Zacchaeus in you. Give this passage time to do its work in you.

The verb translated here: 'I must stay' is the same verb as in John's Gospel, chapter 15. It means to 'abide', or 'indwell', or 'be in close and settled union with'; an experience that seems to us in our persistent self-centredness a very long way off.

So, like Zacchaeus up his tree, hidden away amongst the branches and peering from afar, we gaze wistfully on at the strong and saintly lives of others, unnoticed.

Yet the degree to which we are still is the degree to which we are hurrying down . . .

. . . and opening doors to someone different.

Do not take pleasure in a multiplicity of psalms. It casts a veil over your heart. A single word in intimacy is worth more than a thousand at a distance.

Evagrius of Pontus [91]

Third Sunday before Advent

Stilling and Centring

Take time to be still. Use a verse from the psalm, or a word or phrase you have chosen, or follow your own path into stillness and adoration.

Psalm 17:8   *Keep me as the apple of your eye,*
hide me under the shadow of your wings.

Offering

Offer your day and your concerns that you may be 'kept' through all that you have to do.

Reflecting

Reflect on Luke 6:20-26. *(This Gospel is set for All Saints' Sunday in Year C, and is chosen in preference to the one for the third before Advent.)*

Here is the less well-known version of the Beatitudes, four as opposed to Matthew's eight, with four contrasting woes to the rich and self-sufficient.

Jesus is not speaking of the state of being in poverty, hunger or grief as being in itself 'blessed', nor of being rich as in itself bad. Rather he focuses on an attitude of profound humble-heartedness, the acknowledgement of our need and hunger for God, as being the only path into the wealth of the kingdom.

Take these texts into your heart; pray them deeply.

These paradoxical phrases up-end the world's understandings and give clues to God's artful ways of transforming image into likeness. And the Church is his workshop, a community for the practising of the meanings that make us, a place for celebrating our slow becoming.

The more you stop hiding and own up to having need;
the more the defended hearts of others will open to you –
and you are blessed;

and the more you are blessed amongst others
and find spontaneity,
and the capacity to love and be poor;

the more you know who you are, a daughter or son of God,
for whom life is no longer a reward earned
but a gift amazingly given.

This is the impossible kingdom that lures us. We are encouraged to step out, from behind all protections . . .

. . . into the vulnerable process of being made.

We become contemplatives when God discovers himself in us.

Thomas Merton [92]

Second Sunday before Advent

Stilling and Centring

Take time to be still. Use a phrase from the psalm, or a word or phrase you have chosen, or follow your own path into stillness and adoration.

Psalm 119:105   *Your word is a lantern to my feet*
and a light upon my path.

Offering

Offer your journey of faith for this day, this week, that you may learn what it means to 'endure' in faith. Offer those whose faith is tested by persecution, pain, grief or loss, and for whom the word 'endurance' is all too real.

Reflecting

During the week reflect on Luke 21:5-19.

A complex passage referring to the destruction of the Temple, apocalyptic beliefs current at the time, and the experience of persecution in the early Church. At first sight it all seems very foreign to us. Nevertheless, at its heart the focus is ever contemporary: holding to God and aware of the life of the Spirit day by day, come what may. It is an enduring message which we can interpret in our very different world.

In the mysterious chemistry of spirituality, the gift of 'soul' is given only over time.

We 'gain' our souls – our very selves, as we learn to 'endure'.

Ghandi was known as the 'Mahatma', meaning 'great soul'. By silence, fasting, and repetition of the name of God, that tiny man, following the way of the sermon on the mount, became great.

The journey may be lifelong . . . but each day a small advance.

Without worship you shrink, it is as brutal as that.

Peter Schaeffer [93]

Christ the King

Stilling and Centring

Take time to be still. Use a phrase from the psalm, or a word or phrase you have chosen, or follow your own path into stillness and adoration.

Psalm 46:11   *Be still, and know that I am God.*

Offering

On this last day of the Church's year, spend some time offering your life, your time, your gifts, yourself as a member of a family, of a church community, of a country, and of a world. Try to spend some time during the coming Advent in a more extended reflection, looking at your practice of prayer, perhaps with the help of a spiritual director or soul friend. Offer your time and your plans for the coming day or week.

Reflecting

During the week reflect on Luke 23:33-43.

From the cross comes the infinitely compassionate judgement on us all in our arrogance, violence and pride, which alienates us even from ourselves so that 'we do not know what we are doing'.

On this last Sunday of the year, give yourself time to ponder this passage deeply. We are all these people who surround Jesus Christ.

To pray is to turn,

weeping,

and make a long journey home from a far off country

and to know again what we are doing;

to be held by love's agony

and to gaze in wonder,

as we find ourselves

seamlessly integrated into the merciful

Oneness of God,

bursting open

like a flower of Paradise

within us.

All of us who are human beings are in the image of God. But to be in his likeness belongs only to those who by great love have attached their freedom to God.

Diadochus of Photike [94]

On the last day we shall be judged by our love.

St John of the Cross [95]

RESOURCES FOR THE
CONTINUING JOURNEY OF PRAYER

In addition to the works that are specifically cited in the references, any good religious bookshop will have useful publications in the field of contemplative spirituality. There is no substitute for browsing to find what seems personally helpful. Here are two directions for further reading that may be particularly fruitful:

- The writings of the Benedictine monk John Main, and Laurence Freeman his successor, have inspired the development of the World Community of Christian Meditation. This community, which publishes a regular newsletter, organises conferences and retreats and supports a network of meditators and meditation groups across the UK and the world. It has helped large numbers of people discover a simple 'mantra' style of contemplative prayer that has its roots in the tradition of the early Church.

   Address: 23 Kennington Square, London, W8 5HN

   Tel: 020 7937 4679

   Fax: 020 7937 6790

   email: LondonCentre@wccm.freeserve.co.uk

   website: www.wccm.org

- Some may be helped by exploring the work of the American Cistercian monk and contemplative Thomas Merton; this continues to be an inspiration to huge numbers of people. Merton wrote prolifically and there is also a large amount of literature published about him. There is now a Thomas Merton Society of Great Britain and Ireland, which holds conferences and publishes a quarterly journal.

   Website for all information on the Society:

   http://stop.@/thomasmerton/

REFERENCES

1   Jim Forest, *Praying with Icons*, Orbis Books, 1997, p. 30.

2   William Blake, quoted in Laurence Freeman, *Web of Silence*, DLT, 1996, p. 74.

3   St Augustine, quoted in Laurence Freeman, *Web of Silence*, p. 75.

4   Gregory of Nyssa, 'Homilies on the Song of Songs, 8' (*Patrologia Graeca*, Migne 44, 940-41). Quoted in Olivier Clément, *The Roots of Christian Mysticism*, New City, 1993, p. 240.

5   Alexander Solzhenitsyn, quoted in Michael Mayne, *This Sunrise of Wonder*, Fount, 1995, p. 47.

6   Paul Eluard, from Patrick White, *The Solid Mandala*, Penguin, 1969. (Quoted in Michael Mayne, *This Sunrise of Wonder*, Fount, 1995, p. 67)

7   Edward Robinson, *The Original Vision: Religious Experience of Childhood*, pp. 32-33, The Religious Experience Research Unit, 1977. (Quoted in Ramon SSF, *The Flame of Sacred Love*, BRF, pp. 71-72)

8   Mark Rutherford, *More Pages from a Journal*, Oxford, 1910. (Quoted in Michael Mayne, *This Sunrise of Wonder*, Fount, 1995, p. 37)

9   Quoted in a lecture 'Re-enchanting the Bourgeois Mind' given in Wells Cathedral by Melvyn Matthews, 1998.

10   Thomas Merton, *Conjectures of a Guilty Bystander*, Burns and Oates, 1968, pp. 140-41.

11   Gerard Manley Hopkins, *The Grandeur of God*, Poems and Prose Penguin, 1953, p. 27.

12   Words of Basil of Caesarea, quoted by Gregory Nazianzen, 'Eulogy of Basil the Great', Oration 43, 48 (*Patrologia Graeca*, Migne 36, 560). Quoted in Olivier Clément, *The Roots of Christian Mysticism*, New City, 1993, p. 76.

13   Irenaeus of Lyons, 'Against Heresies', IV, 20, 7 (*Sources Chretiennes*, Cerf, Paris, pp. 153, 186-88). Quoted in Olivier Clément, *The Roots of Christian Mysticism*, New City, 1993, p. 265.

14   Margaret Hebblethwaite, *Motherhood and God*, Geoffrey Chapman, 1984, pp. 110-11.

15   Thomas Merton, *Seeds of Contemplation*, Anthony Clarke Books, 1972, p. 51.

16   Thomas Merton, 'The Inner Experience. Notes on Contemplation' (Unpublished). Quoted in James Finlay, *Merton's Palace of Nowhere*, Ave Maria Press, 1978, p. 91.

17   Thomas Merton, *Contemplative Prayer*, DLT, 1973, p. 33.

18   Anon, *The Cloud of Unknowing*, Penguin, 1961, p. 60.

19 Michael Mayne, *This Sunrise of Wonder*, Fount, 1995, p. 285.

20 Dom John Chapman, 'Spiritual Letters', quoted in Paul Harris, *The Fire of Silence and Stillness*, DLT, 1995, p. 153.

21 Simone Weil, *Waiting on God*, Collins, 1950, p.177.

22 Robert E. Kennedy, *Zen Spirit, Christian Spirit*, Continuum Publishing Company, 1998, p. 55.

A Guide for a Year of Contemplative Prayer

23 T. S. Eliot, *Collected Poems 1909-1962*, 'East Coker', *The Four Quartets*. Faber and Faber, 1963.

24 Pseudo-Macarius, 'Coptic Cycle of Sayings' (*Annales du Musee Guimet* XXV, p. 160). Quoted in Olivier Clément, *The Roots of Christian Mysticism*, New City, 1993, p. 205.

25 Jim Forest, *Praying with Icons*, Orbis Books, 1997, p. 32.

26 David Jenkins, *Still Living with Questions*, SCM, 1990, p. 167.

27 Richard Jefferies, *The Story of My Heart*, Chapter 5. (Quoted in Patrick Grant, *A Dazzling Darkness*, Fount, 1985, pp. 72-73)

28 Thomas Merton, *Seeds of Contemplation*, Anthony Clarke Books, 1972, p. 28.

29 Meister Eckhart, 'Sermons'. (Quoted in Oliver Davies, *God Within*, DLT, 1988, pp. 55-56)

30 Athanasius of Alexandria, *Life of Anthony*. (Quoted in Olivier Clément, *The Roots of Christian Mysticism*, New City, 1993, p. 204)

31 Simone Weil, quoted in Susan White, *A Spirit of Worship*, DLT, 1995, p. 89.

32 Gregory Nazianzen, 'Oration 45, For Easter, 7' (*Patrologia Graeca*, Migne, 36, 850). Quoted in Olivier Clément, *The Roots of Christian Mysticism*, New City, 1993, p. 77.

33 Gregory Mayers, *Listen to the Desert*, Burns and Oates, 1997, p. 47.

34 Theophan the Recluse, *The Art of Prayer, an Orthodox Anthology*, Faber and Faber, 1966, p. 127.

35 Evelyn Underhill, *Mysticism*, Methuen and Co, 1911, p. 325.

36 Gregory of Nyssa, 'Homilies on the Beatitudes, 6' (*Patrologia Graeca* 44, 1270). Quoted in Olivier Clément, *The Roots of Christian Mysticism*, New City, 1993, p. 237.

37 Augustine of Hippo, quoted in Laurence Freeman, *Web of Silence*, DLT, 1996, p. 75.

38 Augustine of Hippo, 'Sermons, 23, 7' (*Patrologia Latina*, Migne, 38, 157). Quoted in Olivier Clément, *The Roots of Christian Mysticism*, New City, 1993, p. 249.

39 John Chrysostom, quoted in Susan White, *A Spirit of Worship*, DLT, 1995, p. 55.

40   R. S. Thomas, 'The Kingdom', *Collected Poems 1945-90*, Phoenix Giants, p. 233.

41   Gregory Mayers, *Listen to the Desert*, Burns and Oates, 1997, p. 52.

42   Johannes Tauler, Sermon 31. (Quoted in Oliver Davies, ed., *The Rhineland Mystics*, SPCK, 1989, p. 71)

43   Hesychius of Batos, 'On Sobriety and Virtue' (156 *Philokalia I*, 165). Quoted in Olivier Clément, *The Roots of Christian Mysticism*, New City, 1993, p. 209.

44   Evelyn Underhill, *Mysticism*, Methuen and Co, 1911, p. 302.

45   Gregory Mayers, *Listen to the Desert*, Burns and Oates, 1997, p. 53.

46   Jim Forest, *Praying with Icons*, Orbis Books, 1997, p. 30.

47   Olivier Clément, *The Roots of Christian Mysticism*, New City, 1993, p. 184.

48   Anon, *The Cloud of Unknowing*, Penguin, 1961, p. 60.

49   Olivier Clément, *The Roots of Christian Mysticism*, New City, 1993, p. 234.

50   Laurence Freeman, *Web of Silence*, DLT, 1996, p. 108.

51   Terry Tastard, *The Spark in the Soul*, p.75.

52   Pseudo-Macarius, 'Thirty-Third Homily' (*Patrologia Graeca* 34, 741). Quoted in Olivier Clément, *The Roots of Christian Mysticism*, New City, 1993, p. 185.

53   Robert E. Kennedy, *Zen Spirit, Christian Spirit*, Continuum Publishing Company, 1998, p. 41.

54   Hugh Lavery, *Reflections*, Mayhew McCrimmon, 1978, p. 68. (Quoted in Michael Mayne, *This Sunrise of Wonder*, Fount, p. 280)

55   Olivier Clément, *The Roots of Christian Mysticism*, New City, 1993, p. 273.

56   Odes of Solomon, 17 (Harris-Mingana, pp. 289-90). Quoted in Olivier Clément, *The Roots of Christian Mysticism*, New City, 1993, p. 52.

57   Olivier Clément, *The Roots of Christian Mysticism*, New City, 1993, p. 226.

58   Olivier Clément, *The Roots of Christian Mysticism*, New City, 1993, p. 236.

59   Gerard W. Hughes, *God Where are You?*, DLT, 1997, p. 192.

60   R. S. Thomas, 'The Kingdom', *Collected Poems 1945-90*, Phoenix Giants, p. 166.

61   Thomas Merton, 'In conversation', 1968, quoted in Paul Harris, *The Fire of Silence and Stillness*, DLT, 1995, pp. 102-3.

62   Thomas Merton, *The Wisdom of the Desert*, Burns and Oates, 1997, pp. 48-49.

63   John Updike, *Self-consciousness*, Penguin, 1990. (Quoted in Michael Mayne, *This Sunrise of Wonder*, Fount, 1995, p. 62)

64 Benedict of Nursia, *Rule VII* (*Centenario*, pp. 32-42). Quoted in Olivier Clément, *The Roots of Christian Mysticism*, New City, 1993, p. 156.

65 Margaret Miles, 'The Discovery of Asceticism', (*Commonweal CX*, January 1983: 40, 43). Quoted in Robert E. Kennedy, *Zen Spirit, Christian Spirit*, Continuum Publishing Company, 1998, p. 101.

66 Terry Tastard, *The Spark in the Soul*, p. 76.

67 Olivier Clément, *The Roots of Christian Mysticism*, New City, 1993, p. 230.

68 Anon, *The Cloud of Unknowing*, Penguin, 1961, p. 55-56.

69 Olivier Clément, *The Roots of Christian Mysticism*, New City, 1993, p. 135.

70 Laurence Freeman, *Web of Silence*, DLT, 1996, p. 68.

71 Galatians 2:20.

72 Pseudo-Macarius, 'Thirty-Third Homily' (*Patrologia Graeca* 34, 741). Quoted in Olivier Clément, *The Roots of Christian Mysticism*, New City, 1993, p. 184.

73 Llewellyn Vaughan-Lee, *Sufism: The Transformation of the Heart*, The Golden Sufi Center, 1995, p. 64.

74 Diadochus of Photike, 'Gnostic Chapters, 59' (*Sources Chretiennes*, Cerf, Paris 5 bis, p. 119). Quoted in Olivier Clément, *The Roots of Christian Mysticism*, New City, 1993, p. 206.

75 Thomas Traherne, 'Centuries of Meditation, IV. 95'. (Quoted in Patrick Grant, *A Dazzling Darkness*, Fount, 1985, p. 246)

76 Diadochus of Photike, 'Gnostic Chapters, Preamble' (*Sources Chretiennes*, Cerf, Paris 5 bis, pp. 84-85). Quoted in Olivier Clément, *The Roots of Christian Mysticism*, New City, 1993, p. 139.

77 Gregory Mayers, *Listen to the Desert*, Burns and Oates, 1997, p. 87.

78 Philip Toynbee, 'Part of a Journey. Entry for 15 February 1978.' (Quoted in Michael Mayne, *This Sunrise of Wonder*, Fount, 1995, p. 81)

79 Basil of Caesarea, 'Treatise on the Holy Spirit, 27' (*Patrologia Graeca* 32, 192). Quoted in Olivier Clément, *The Roots of Christian Mysticism*, New City, 1993, p. 197.

80 Gregory Nazianzen, 'Oration 45, For Easter, 9' (*Patrologia Graeca* 36, 851-52). Quoted in Olivier Clément, *The Roots of Christian Mysticism*, New City, 1993, p. 88.

81 Theophilus of Antioch, 'Three Books to Autolycus', quoted in Olivier Clément, *The Roots of Christian Mysticism*, New City, 1993, p. 73.

82 Robert E. Kennedy, *Zen Spirit, Christian Spirit*, Continuum Publishing Company, 1998, p. 72.

83   Origen, 'Homily on Genesis, I, 4' (*Griechische Christliche Schriftsteller*, Berlin, 6, 113-21). Quoted in Olivier Clément, *The Roots of Christian Mysticism*, New City, 1993, p. 131.

84   Thomas Merton, *The Ascent to Truth*, Burns and Oates, 1951, p. 39.

85   Olivier Clément, *The Roots of Christian Mysticism*, New City, 1993, p. 250.

86   Augustine of Hippo, 'Confessions, IX, X, 23-5' (*Belles Lettres* p. 227-29). Quoted in Olivier Clément, *The Roots of Christian Mysticism*, New City, 1993, p. 232.

87   Michael Mayne, *This Sunrise of Wonder*, Fount, 1995, p. 280.

88   Gregory Mayers, *Listen to the Desert*, Burns and Oates, 1997, p. 15.

89   R. S. Thomas, 'The Kingdom', *Collected Poems 1945-90*, Phoenix Giants, p. 199.

90   Dietrich Bonhoeffer, *The Narrow Path*, quoted in Paul Harris, *The Fire of Silence and Stillness*, DLT, 1995, p. 98.

91   Evagrius of Pontus, 'Pareneticus' (*Frankenberg*, p. 561). Quoted in Olivier Clément, *The Roots of Christian Mysticism*, New City, 1993, p. 201-2.

92   Thomas Merton, *Seeds of Contemplation*, Anthony Clarke Books, 1972, p. 31.

93   Peter Schaeffer, *Equus*. (Quoted in Susan White, *A Spirit of Worship*, DLT, 1995, p. 34)

94   Diadochus of Photike, 'Gnostic Chapters, 4' (*Sources Chretiennes*, 5 bis, p. 86). Quoted in Olivier Clément, *The Roots of Christian Mysticism*, New City, 1993, p. 90.

95   St John of the Cross, quoted in Olivier Clément, *The Roots of Christian Mysticism*, New City, 1993, p. 274.

ACKNOWLEDGEMENTS AND ADDRESSES FOR PUBLISHERS OF CITED BOOKS

The publishers wish to express their gratitude to the following for permission to include copyright material in this publication:

Continuum International Publishing Group Ltd, Wellington House, 125 Strand, London, WC2R 0BB, for the extracts from *Listen to the Desert* by Gregory Mayers (1997), *The Wisdom of the Desert* by Thomas Merton (1997) and *Conjectures of a Guilty Bystander* by Thomas Merton (1968), all published by Burns & Oates. Also *Motherhood and God* by Margaret Hebblethwaite (1984).

Continuum International Publishing Group Ltd, 370 Lexington Avenue, New York, NY 10017-6503, USA, for the extracts taken from *Zen Spirit, Christian Spirit* by Robert E. Kennedy, © Copyright 1995 Robert E. Kennedy.

Darton Longman & Todd Ltd, 1 Spencer Court, 140-142 Wandsworth High Street, London, SW18 4JJ, for the extracts taken from *The Spark in the Soul* by Terry Tastard, published and © 1989 Darton, Longman & Todd Ltd, *Contemplative Prayer* by Thomas Merton, published and © 1975 Darton Longman & Todd, *Web of Silence* by Laurence Freeman, published and © 1996 Darton Longman & Todd Ltd, and *God, Where Are You?* by Gerard W. Hughes, © 1997 Darton Longman & Todd. Used by permission of the publishers.

Faber & Faber Ltd, 3 Queens Square, London, WC1N 3AU, for the extract from 'East Coker', *The Four Quartets* by T. S. Eliot, taken from *Collected Poems 1909-1962*, Faber & Faber 1963.

HarperCollins Publishers, 77-85 Fulham Palace Road, London, W6 8JB, for the extract from *This Sunrise of Wonder* by Michael Mayne.

Laurence Pollinger Ltd, 18 Maddox Street, Mayfair, London, W1R 0EU, for the extract from *Bonhoeffer – True Patriot* by Mary Bosanquet.

McCrimmon Publishing Co Ltd, 10-12 High Street, Great Wakering, Essex, SS3 0EQ, for the extract from *Reflections* by Hugh Lavery, © McCrimmon Publishing Co Ltd.

New City, 57 Twyford Avenue, London, W3 9PZ, for the extracts taken from *The Roots of Christian Mysticism* by Olivier Clément (1993).

Orbit Books, PO Box 308, Maryknoll, New York 10545-0308, USA, for the extracts taken from *Praying with Icons* by Jim Forest (1997).

Orion Publishing Group Ltd, Orion House, 5 Upper Saint Martin's Lane, London, WC2H 9EA, for the extracts taken from *Collected Poems 1945-90* by R. S. Thomas.

Penguin UK, 27 Wrights Lane, London, W8 5TZ, for the extract from *Self-consciousness* by John Updike. Penguin Books 1990.

Tessa Sayle Agency, 11 Jubilee Place, London, SW3 3TE, for the extract from *Mysticism* by Evelyn Underhill, published by Methuen & Co, 1911.

SCM Press, 9-17 St. Albans Place, London, N1 0NX, for the extract from *Still Living with Questions* by David Jenkins (1990).

The Golden Sufi Centre, PO Box 428, Inverness, California 94937-0428, USA, for the extract from *The Transformation of the Heart* by Llewellyn Vaughan-Lee, © The Golden Sufi Centre 1995.

Most of the Psalms in this publication are taken from the *Standard Book of Common Prayer of the Episcopal Church in the USA*.

The remaining Psalms are taken from the Psalter of the *Alternative Service Book* and are © HarperCollins Publishers.

181

SUNDAYS OF THE YEAR (3-YEAR LECTIONARY)

The Sundays of the Church's year are celebrated on different dates each year. This chart will tell you how the Sundays of the year correspond with the calendar dates. Find the date in the dates column, then look to the left and the chart will tell you which Sunday of the year is being celebrated. You can then use the appropriate page of the Guide.

	2000/2001 YEAR C	2001/2002 YEAR A	2002/2003 YEAR B
ADVENT 1	3/12/00	2/12/01	1/12/02
ADVENT 2	10/12/00	9/12/01	8/12/02
ADVENT 3	17/12/00	16/12/01	15/12/02
ADVENT 4	24/12/00	23/12/01	22/12/02
CHRISTMAS DAY	25/12/00	25/12/01	25/12/02
CHRISTMAS 1	31/12/00	30/12/01	29/12/02
CHRISTMAS 2			5/1/03
EPIPHANY		6/1/02	
EPIPHANY 1/BAPTISM OF CHRIST	7/1/01		12/1/03
EPIPHANY 2	14/1/01	13/1/02	19/1/03
EPIPHANY 3	21/1/01	20/1/02	26/1/03
EPIPHANY 4	28/1/01	27/1/02	2/2/03 Presentation of Christ
5TH BEFORE LENT			
4TH BEFORE LENT	4/2/01		9/2/03
3RD BEFORE LENT	11/2/01		16/2/03
2ND BEFORE LENT	18/2/01	3/2/02	23/2/03
SUNDAY NEXT BEFORE LENT	25/2/01	10/2/02	2/3/03
LENT 1	4/3/01	17/2/02	9/3/03
LENT 2	11/3/01	24/2/02	16/3/03
LENT 3	18/3/01	3/3/02	23/3/03
LENT 4	25/3/01	10/3/02	30/3/03
LENT 5 (PASSION SUNDAY)	1/4/01	17/3/02	6/4/03
PALM SUNDAY	8/4/01	24/3/02	13/4/03
EASTER DAY	15/4/01	31/3/02	20/4/03
EASTER 2	22/4/01	7/4/02	27/4/03
EASTER 3	29/4/01	14/4/02	4/5/03

	2000/2001 Year C	2001/2002 Year A	2002/2003 Year B
Easter 4	6/5/01	21/4/02	11/5/03
Easter 5	13/5/01	28/4/02	18/5/03
Easter 6	20/5/01	5/5/02	25/5/03
Easter 7	27/5/01	12/5/02	1/6/03
Pentecost	3/6/01	19/5/02	8/6/03
Trinity	10/6/01	26/5/02	15/6/03
1st after Trinity	17/6/01	2/6/02	22/6/03
2nd after Trinity	24/6/01	9/6/02	29/6/03
3rd after Trinity	1/7/01	16/6/02	6/7/03
4th after Trinity	8/7/01	23/6/02	13/7/03
5th after Trinity	15/7/01	30/6/02	20/7/03
6th after Trinity	22/7/01	7/7/02	27/7/03
7th after Trinity	29/7/01	14/7/02	3/8/03
8th after Trinity	5/8/01	21/7/02	10/8/03
9th after Trinity	12/8/01	28/7/02	17/8/03
10th after Trinity	19/8/01	4/8/02	24/8/03
11th after Trinity	26/8/01	11/8/02	31/8/03
12th after Trinity	2/9/01	18/8/02	7/9/03
13th after Trinity	9/9/01	25/8/02	14/9/03
14th after Trinity	16/9/01	1/9/02	21/9/03
15th after Trinity	23/9/01	8/9/02	28/9/03
16th after Trinity	30/9/01	15/9/02	5/10/03
17th after Trinity	7/10/01	22/9/02	12/10/03
18th after Trinity	14/10/01	29/9/02	19/10/03
19th after Trinity	21/10/01	6/10/02	
20th after Trinity		13/10/02	
21st after Trinity		20/10/02	
22nd after Trinity			
Last after Trinity	28/10/01	27/11/02	26/10/03
4th before Advent	4/11/01	3/11/02	2/11/03
3rd before Advent	11/11/01	10/11/02	9/11/03
2nd before Advent	18/11/01	17/11/02	16/11/03
Christ the King	25/11/01	24/11/02	23/11/03